A Runner's Tale
Six Decades on the Road

Joe Oakes

Piano! Piano! Press
Portland, OR

ISBN: 978-0-615-74424-7

Text set in Adobe Garamond Pro
Cover and book design by John Morris-Reihl, www.artntech.com
Manufactured by Lightning Source, LLC

DEDICATION

This book is dedicated to all the runners
Who take that first sometimes difficult running
step out the front door
On hot days, cold days, fair weather or foul.

It is also dedicated to the coaches, who for little
Monetary return, dedicate hours and years of their lives
Encouraging young people and teaching them to love this sport.
I must single out a wonderful man, my own first coach,
now long gone,

Coach Howie Borck.

"It is not the critic who counts, not the man who points out how the strong man stumbled – or where the doer of deeds could have done better – the credit belongs to the man who is actually in the arena – whose face is marked by dust and sweat and blood – who strives valiantly, who knows the great enthusiasm, the great devotion, and spends himself in a worthy cause – who at the best knows in the end the triumph of high achievement and who at the worst, if he fails, at least fails while doing greatly – so that his place shall never be with those cold and timid souls who know neither victory nor defeat."

– Theodore Roosevelt

On first reading, TR comes off sounding like an elitist, a cheerleading hero worshipper. His image of "those cold and timid souls who know neither victory nor defeat" sounds like a condemnation of anyone who does not force himself valiantly and painfully into the death throes of battle. Surely, not everyone is of a competitive or combative nature. Still, TR still gives us a lot to think about. We do feel good about the one who has put forth their maximum effort, win or lose. We heap adulation on winners. And don't we think less of the slacker who, in the heat of a competition, slinks to the background when the team really needs everyone's best effort?

We cannot all be as heroic and admired as someone like Manny Paquiao, the great Philippine boxer, simultaneous holder of world boxing championship titles in seven weight classes. But each of us can honorably offer the best that is within us. There is great value in striving for a lofty goal. That is especially true in the sport of running, where it is the expenditure of an individual's effort that determines the final result.

At the same time, if we look at running merely as competition we are missing a few very important dimensions of the sport. There is joy and beauty in running, whether we are racing or running alone on a remote trail. There is physical connectedness of feet to the face of earth, body moving across the planet. And there is the private communication with my inner self and maybe with my higher power.

Rejoice in all that running means to you!

ILLUSTRATIONS

A Memoir of Six Decades of Running

"One's destination is never a place, but a new way of seeing things."
  – Henry Miller
"Never let an adventure pass you by."
  – Joan Lunden

Every day holds an adventure, and every turn in the path presents something new to me. Yesterday it was a pair of young black tail bucks, one on each side of the narrow Wildwood trail in Forest Park. I stopped running to let them decide what to do. They seemed confused, each waiting for the other to decide which way to go. Then they darted off into the trees in opposite directions, gone. Today's small encounter was in the Nature Park with a fat, slow salamander. He was following his urges, making his once-a-year trip to a place where, I presume, he will meet his salamander sweetie to provide tomorrow's world with new salamanders. I guess once a year is enough if you are a salamander.

When I meet these new friends I wait; I have the luxury of not being in a hurry. I have done enough hurrying. Now I can take my time and more fully enjoy the world as it unfolds in front of me. I don't want to miss any of it.

PREFACE

IT IS CROSS COUNTRY SEASON, OCTOBER 1948. There is a long line of skinny teenage runners stretching north and south in a line parallel to Broadway, waiting for the starter's pistol to explode. We are all facing east in a huge, open field in Van Cortland Park in the northwest Bronx, hundreds of us, from every high school in the area. A quarter of a mile in front of us is a narrow opening to a dusty trail that will take us into the hills. The runners who reach that opening first will have a big advantage: All other runners will have to eat the dust kicked up by the front runners, and the further back you are, the more dust will be in the air. Once on the trail, passing is going to be very difficult. The best strategy is to sprint that first quarter mile across the field, get to the opening early, then hang on for the rest of the two and a quarter mile race. I am choking on dust in the middle of the pack, in a better position than I expected. Muscling up hills and tearing wildly downhill I manage to squeeze past a handful of runners. As I near the end of the race there, again, is that big, open field. A quarter mile in front of me is the finish line, with coaches, team-mates and family jumping up and down and screaming. It is time for me to pour my guts out. I dig deep and deeper and deeper still, forcing myself to run the last 200 yards like a sprinter. Right here and right now a runner discovers what he is really made of. This is the 1948 Bronx-Manhattan-Westchester high school cross country championships, and I am competing in my first really big race.

Flash forward 64 years to the autumn of 2012, just past of my 77th birthday. After all these years, I am still running, more or less (more of the less, to be honest.) I am on the 1.93 mile loop surrounding the Beaverton, Oregon campus of the Nike Corporation, mostly wood chips, easy on my aging knees. It is one of three lovely and calming places in the area where I can indulge in what is left of my declining running addiction. I am fully present, enjoying my surroundings. There are ducks, geese and songbirds, and across the pond a nutria is swimming, mostly submerged. But I find myself drawn into the past. As I run, slowly and sometimes painfully, I divert myself with delightful memories of running so long ago in Van Cortland Park and so many other places that have brought me years of joy and occasional success. *Today, after six decades, I can close my eyes and clearly see the narrow opening across that big field in Van Cortland Park; I am still sprinting towards the opening; the dirt and rocks and roots of the trail are as real to me as they were then. I hear the crowd screaming their heads off at the finish line, almost choking on the dust in my dry mouth, see the vivid flash of colors of the singlets in front of me, among them the proud 'cardinal and gold' of my own Cardinal Hayes High School team. I feel myself desperately trying to suck in enough air to carry me the last few hundred yards. Once again, I am there.*

Inside of me are so many wonderful memories waiting to be set loose. I hope that you will allow me to share some of them with you.

Table of Contents

A Man in His Underwear

"I can't change the direction of the wind, but I can adjust my sails to reach my destination."
– Jimmy Dean

"Every noble work is at first impossible."
– Carlyle

"Being afraid to take chances means never exploring the possibilities. If you never explore the possibilities, you may miss out on your once in a lifetime chance."
– Bridgett Middleton

We can't change the direction of the wind and we can't stop the inexorable march of the clock and the calendar. So why worry about it? I am no longer able to do what was easy at 18, but I can put my 78 year old body through whatever paces it can handle. The choice is simple: moan and groan about your losses or celebrate what you have, even in the certain knowledge that tomorrow you will have a little less. I think that I enjoy my aging physical self more than my former, highly energetic 18 year old self enjoyed himself. He/I didn't know very much. What can you possibly know at 18?

CHAPTER 1
A MAN IN HIS UNDERWEAR

Luck is a constant companion to all of us, be it good luck or bad. When I look back at my life I see a predominance of good fortune, much of it arriving in the form of people who brought joy into my life and were instrumental in reaching goals that I could not have imagined.

One of those people was Howie Borck. Mister Borck was the track coach at Cardinal Hayes High School in The Bronx. I met him when I was a 135 pound freshman who thought that I could play football with guys like Paul Baroncelli, a gentle giant who had a 100 pound advantage on me. I was convinced that I was pretty tough after winning two out of three Golden Gloves fights. (I got my ass royally kicked in the third one.) Coach Borck was at football practice scouting for sprinters for his track team. He rescued me from my unrealistic football fantasy and he told me that he could train me to be a distance runner. In my mind running track was for sissies. But I thought that maybe it would be good training for any other real sport, even football, so I decided to give it a shot. That September 1948 decision was the first step in a lifetime of running, one that has lasted for 64 years so far.

I loved Coach Borck back then and I still do, though he is long gone. He was a man who could draw the most out of a boy by giving relaxed, positive direction. He never raised his voice, but he was always nearby to observe and make suggestions. When you did something that pleased him, he was effusive with his praise. When you goofed up, he quietly showed how you might have done better. It was very important to him that his runners keep things in perspective. Schoolwork always came before track. If a boy showed signs of injury or fatigue, he made sure that running kept its place well behind healing. I competed with Coach Borck for four years in indoor track in the winter, outdoor track in the spring, and cross country in the fall. I worked hard for him and do not regret a minute of it. He taught us to set goals and to work honestly to reach them. Those lessons has proven to be of great value to me and has guided me throughout my life.

And our team was a team. Track is an individual sport, but Coach Borck had us look after each other. One team member's victory was a win for all of us. Our school did not have our own track, so we travelled from place to place to practice. The school gym was a basketball court, not a good place to run. In the spring we used the outdoor cinder track at McComb's Dam Park, across from Yankee Stadium, about a mile from the school. We had no cars or school buses to transport us, so we did our warm-up runs on the way to the track. In the fall we took the subway to Van Cortland Park to train on the cross-country loop. In the winter we sometimes worked out at the indoor Fordham Skating Rink, about 20 laps to the mile (we all suffered from shin-splints), and maybe at the Kingsbridge Armory if it was available.

FLASHBACK: September, 1950. Jim Tobin and I are in the south wing of L-shaped Cardinal Hayes High School, peering around the corner to see if 'Jabo' is at his post at the main entrance to the school, at the middle door. His office is there and he monitors traffic coming in and out. Father Stanislaus Jablonski is the Dean of Discipline and if there is one thing he loves more than catching smokers, it is catching students sneaking out of school early. Jabo is sitting in his office, so we should be able to escape. Tobin and I leave through the unguarded south door, make it across the Grand Concourse and into Carl Schurz Park. We run downhill across the park, through a few streets and we are at the vendor's entrance to Yankee Stadium. We are not too late.

These are great years for the Yankees. Joe DiMaggio, Yogi Berra, Allie Reynolds, Phil Rizzuto, Whitey Ford (then Mickey Mantle and later Roger Maris) are huge drawing cards. But Tobin and I are not here to see a baseball game. We are at Yankee Stadium to work.

The Yankees are doing well, and today's game against Boston should be a good one for us, but first we will have put in the required slave labor. Vendors (peanuts, popcorn, cold drinks, souvenir baseballs, "Ya can't tell da the players widout a scorecard," "Hey, getcha cold beer here.") are mostly kids and we have to put in an hour or so packing peanuts into nickel paper sacks. We will not be paid for that work. However, if we do not 'volunteer' to do it, we will probably not be selected as vendors that day by the Harry M. Stevens Company, the people who own the concessions at Yankee Stadium and most of the major league ball parks.

Tobin calls our gang the Hungry Highbridge Hustlers. He gets to sell soda today from a hose attached a metal backpack tank that dispenses the soda into paper cups. It is hard work, but it is a hot day and he should sell a lot of soda. I start out selling scorecards and souvenir baseballs and do okay. After the third inning I transform into a hot dog peddler. That is much better because as the afternoon goes on the fans are getting hungry. The less ambitious vendors just walk the horizontal aisles picking off easy customers. A real hustler will spend the afternoon running up and down the concrete steps to reach the people at the top. Up there they appreciate your climb and a few will give a dime tip. (The term for a tip is 'subway'; the price of a ride on the subway is a dime.)

We are not considered employees. We are 'independent contractors.' That way the Harry M. Stevens Company can give us nothing in the way of salary or benefits. If you want to work, you have to earn the privilege, and you are paid only a commission based on what you sell. The more stairs you climb, the more you sell, and the more you earn. I recall one great Sunday double header against the Red Sox when I pocketed $40. That is about what my father could earn for a week of hard work.

I never thought about it then, but running the steps at Yankee Stadium was great training. 'Jabo' never caught us, and that seems *rather odd. I wonder if maybe Father Jablonski was aware that we were sneaking out of school to work and just looked the other way.*

Sometimes the team travelled to track meets. Coach would schedule us for competitions in armories, stadiums, outdoor tracks and even the occasional trip to places like West Point, where, in 1949 we defeated the US Military Academy freshman squad in a dual meet. Coach Borck trained me to run half mile and mile races in both indoor and outdoor seasons. I loved running cross country in the fall, but I think that my favorite events were the mile and two mile relays. I remember winning gold at a meet in Randall's Island Stadium with Danny Roselli, Jimmy Mahon and Patrick O'Leary on our two-mile relay team. Three of us were leaping up and down like jack-in-the-boxes when Roselli finished the final lap ten yards ahead of the competition. He looked like he was going to die, and we raised him onto our shoulders for a victory lap.

One of my fondest memories was running as a senior in Madison Square Garden, the most famous running venue in New York. It was a big college meet, the Millrose Games, but they had scheduled a few events for high school runners. Coach Borck entered me in the mile. It was on a board track, twelve laps to the mile, banked sharply at both ends. The Garden was filled to capacity, even the balconies. Flood lights illuminated the track, and I can still see the sprinters warming up on the infield, getting ready for the 50 yard dash, skin glowing with perspiration and smelling of liniment. I was scared and very excited. While the sprints were going on we did our warm-ups in the hallway under the stands. When the call came for the mile I took off my cardinal-and-gold sweats, folded them neatly and jogged to the starting line.

There were twelve of us bunched together. I had competed against the guys from Bishop Loughlin and Mount Saint Michael's, both fast milers, but I didn't know the others. I felt strong and con-

5

fident. Coach told me that if I wanted to do well I would have to take it out fast from the beginning to make it difficult for anyone who wanted to pass on the 24 banked turns. Passing on a small, banked track is very hard: there isn't much opportunity on the short straight-aways and it is almost impossible on the banked turns. To pass you have to come off the bank fast and complete your move in the short 35 yard straightaway. Coach reminded me that the guy from Laughlin had a reputation for a strong kick.

Runners to your marks! Get set! The gun cracks and I immediately toss in everything I have, starting at a dead sprint down the first straightaway, grabbing the lead. At the first turn I ease into a pace a bit faster than my comfortable mile pace. No one wants to challenge me for the first six laps. I accelerate hard into each turn, run the curves high, and come off the banks fast and wide, making it tough for anyone to get past me on the outside. 15,000 fans are screaming encouragement to their favorites in our tight pack as we come into the seventh lap. I focus my attention on the yellow-brown board track in front of me, grasping the wood with my spikes and hold onto it as I turn into the next bank. The guy from The Mount makes a bad decision. He tries to pass me high on the bank and goes flying off the track into the wall: one down. The fast start has taken a lot out of me and I am hanging on by the skin of my teeth. I can feel the Loughlin kid laying back in third place, watching me, waiting for the right time to sprint past. His eyes are burning a hole in my back. I can hear his labored breathing. Maybe he is having as hard a time as I am. All of a sudden he turns on the afterburners and blasts by me at the start of the tenth lap. My lungs are on fire and I don't have enough juice left to accelerate and challenge his kick. I am struggling, trying desperately to keep my pace from dropping off. Another rocket-propelled runner burns by me on the final lap, a kid from Power Memorial. Where did he come from? I cross the finish line in third place. No gold, no silver. I gave it my best effort and try not to be disappointed with bronze. Coach Borck gives me a big bear hug and keeps me from collapsing onto the track. Even today, more than 60 years later, I am still not sure whether I was more disappointed about not getting the gold for my team than I am overjoyed that I took a bronze medal doing the best I could.

One of the things that Coach Borck was good at was getting athletic scholarships for his runners. He got me a half scholarship to Manhattan College, one of the best track schools in America at that time. The coach, George Eastman, who had coached the Olympic team, was in the same mold as Howie Borck. But I couldn't afford the other half of the college costs, so I opted to join the Army instead. I figured that maybe when I got out of the Army I could take up where I left off with the financial help of the GI Bill.

There was a war going on in Korea and my brother Richard and I decided that we wanted to jump out of airplanes and go after bad guys. Our father had served in the Army in WWI and our older brothers were WWII veterans. Richard and I volunteered for the Paratroopers because they earned a few dollars more each month and it sounded like fun. But the Army has its own way of doing things, so they sent Richard to Maryland to learn to be a cook, and they sent me to schools to study electronics, communications and Russian language. We put in our time, did not become generals and never got near where the bad guys were. After a couple of years in uniform we returned to civilian life.

During my time in the Army there was no time for running. When I was discharged I decided to study engineering, so I took a day job as an engineering assistant and enrolled in the evening division at the City College of New York (now City U of NY.) I also found Sylvia, the love of my life, and we were married in 1957. Soon I was balancing a full time job, a schedule in the evening engineering school, and a family. Danny was born in 1958.

You may find this hard to believe, but the CCNY night school had a track team. A fellow student, Irv Rattner, a born organizer, corralled a few of us into forming a team. Irv was a slightly built blond with thick glasses and great intensity. Tall, slim Jean Brief was from France, mild-mannered, with a lot of endurance. The hard working Cleary brothers had graduated from my high school, and Egon (who knew everything) was a student from Israel. But how could I possibly find the time to run? I had a job, a family and tough engineering classes to think about. When you really want to do something, you will find the time. We ran on weekends and holidays, sometimes after classes under stadium lights late at night at CCNY's Lewisohn Stadium. And we ran on the cross country course in Van Courtland Park. Irv Rattner even arranged to have our team entered in local meets. Scheduling was difficult, but Irv made it happen. We used to joke that we were the national champions of all night school track teams in the United States: we were probably the only night school track team. I would be very remiss if I did not credit Sylvia for her support and patience during those years.

Here is something that most non-New Yorkers probably do not know. New Yorkers are great walkers. There is a fine subway system and most people use it on a daily basis. But the majority of people live at least a quarter mile from the nearest station, so they walk. When they reach their destination subway stop, there is another walk to get to where they work or to school. It was about two and a half miles from my home to my high school. The 149th Street cross town trolley went most of the way, and it cost only seven and a half cents (later a dime) each way. But unless it was raining or snowing, I walked most days. I liked the exercise and could find better uses for the extra 75 cents each week.

It took forever, but I finally got my engineering degree, then another, and an MBA. Sylvia and I moved our growing family, Danny, Chris and Victoria, from our tiny Bronx apartment to our new home in Merrick, Long Island, a bedroom community not far from New York City. As far as running went, I was now completely on my own. If you are over 60 you are probably aware that in the 1960s *no one* ran after they graduated from school. There were plenty of acceptable things that you could do, like golf, tennis, drinking or bridge, but running was not one of them. That, however, was not going to stop me from doing what I dearly loved. So I ran when and where I could, sometimes in local parks and once in a while on the track at Merrick High School. In cool weather modesty prevailed, and I wore a bulky sweat suit. I remember wearing shorts and a singlet on the Merrick High School track one June afternoon. A neighbor, Nancy Guthie, was passing with six year old, Skippy, and I can still hear little Skippy pointing through the fence and shouting, "Oh, look, Mommy, there is Mister Oakes running around in his underwear."

Times were very different then. Runners were considered weirdos, oddities, and there were very few of us older than school age. We were, in a sense, a small, misunderstood, unappreciated minority. As my life moved forward, I must confess that I let my running slide for a few years. I was doing well in my career. My job involved a lot of travel and it was important for me to spend my limited free time with my young family. In short, living on the road, eating and drinking to excess, I was getting fat.

In 1974 my life took a fortunate turn. I was offered a much better job across the country, in the San Francisco Bay area, as engineering and marketing manager for one of the early high-tech companies in Silicon Valley. We arrived in sunny California in July, and within a week I discovered that the relaxed culture in California was much friendlier to runners than conservative suburban New York.

After high school I joined the Army during the Korean War. This picture is from Basic Combat Infantry Training at Fort Dix, N.J.

These medals from 1948 meant a lot to me as a high school freshman.

High school team mates Danny Roselli, Jimmy Mahon, and John Connally, 1952.

That's me, clowning around during practice, 1951.

CHAPTER TWO

Welcome to California

"Before you criticize anyone, you should walk a mile in their shoes. That way, when you criticize them, you're a mile away and you have their shoes."
– Anonymous

"Avoid meats which angry up the blood. If your stomach disputes you, lie down and pacify it with cool thoughts. Keep the juices flowing by jangling around gently as you move. Go very light on the vices, such as carrying on in society. The social ramble ain't restful. Avoid running at all times. Don't look back. Something might be gaining on you."
– Satchel Paige, How to Stay Young

Where does one find happiness? I was happy enough to be one of eight kids in a small Bronx apartment. I even liked Army life in a cramped barracks lined with bunk beds. Life kept getting better when Sylvia and I moved into to our first house in Long Island, then on to Pennsylvania, California and now, Oregon. It is not so much where you are as whom you are with and what you are doing. Sylvia, my companion for over a half century, has always encouraged me to do the things that brought joy to me, and from the beginning that included running.

How can life be any better than that?

CHAPTER 2
WELCOME TO CALIFORNIA

When we moved to sunny California in the summer of 1974 I was about to turn 40 and had gained a lot of weight. My job had me managing the work of 130 customer engineers located all over the USA, and a few out of the country. On my almost weekly road trips I ate and drank far too much, and I loved it. Entertaining clients and employees was an important part of my job. In August of that year my company sent me in for the physical examination required by the company's insurance provider. The good doctor did all the standard tests, including a blood panel. He frowned and told me that I was not eligible for insurance: I had developed adult onset diabetes, and it was probably the result of the weight I had gained with all that excess eating and drinking. He advised two things: diet and exercise.

Was I upset? You bet I was. Diabetes is an insidious disease. It can be debilitating and sometimes fatal. It also runs in my family. That doctor scared the heck out of me, and there was no question in my mind about taking his advice, starting immediately. Sylvia was immensely helpful in getting me to change my eating habits. How to get my fat body into an exercise program was quite another thing. A co-worker, Constantine Stavropoulos, was a soccer player, and he encouraged me to join him in an industrial league. Our first game was against a Colombian team. Those guys literally ran circles around me. I was flat on my ass more than on my feet. I thought that I would drop dead, not just from embarrassment, but because I was thoroughly bushed. It was clear that I was not ready for soccer or any other rigorous exercise. Constantine politely suggested that I get myself into reasonable physical condition first, then come back and try soccer again. But *how* was I going to get myself fit? It seemed to be way beyond me. But I knew that for me, running was the way to go. I would have to get myself into a running program, but I dreaded the agony and embarrassment of dragging my bulk around a track. I hated my fat body.

Then good fortune presented me with an option. While I was walking with my children on a Sunday morning at nearby Foothill College I saw a group of runners looping around the campus. They were clearly too old to be students. When they finished their work-out I approached sheepishly and found out that they ran there every Sunday morning. They called themselves the Foothill Fun Runners, sponsored by Runner's World Magazine. A peppy, curly-haired, be-spectacled guy named Joe Henderson ran the show. He had a big, winning smile and an honest, friendly face. Henderson told me that this group welcomed beginners and were tolerant of slower runners. "*No matter how slow you are there will always be someone slower,*" he told me, and he was right.

You have to put yourself in my frame of mind: It was 1974, I was a depressed, overweight 40-year-old who had just moved to free-thinking California from a place where a man might be suspected of unnatural behavior if seen running around town in his shorts. *Had I suddenly found myself in Heaven?* The next Sunday morning I showed up to run with them. At first I was self-conscious about my excess weight among the gazelles, but no one else seemed to care about my 'love handles': they were there to run, not run a beauty contest. The weekly format at the Fun Runs started with a warm-up of either a half mile or a quarter mile. Next came a one mile run around the campus loop, and finally the long run of the day, usually five or six miles in the hills. Some of the runners took it easy; others hammered away. For the first month I couldn't make it through the long one and just about jogged through the shorter ones. The other runners were encouraging. In time my weight started to drop and my endurance increased. After a few months the longer runs became easier and I found myself entering local 10 kilometer races. I stopped wearing clothing to hide my fat.

I loved the friendly competition at the Fun Runs. There were two regulars that I tried to keep in my sights in the longer runs, Joe Wakabayashi and teenager Sue Grigsby. Joe ran on short, stubby legs, but he had the stamina of an Arabian stallion. Sue (remember that this was 1974) showed me for the first time that a female runner could kick my macho butt, which she did frequently. She had the long, lean look of a natural distance runner. (Years later, after a successful running career at Cal State, Humboldt, Sue got a job as a track coach at a school in Washington State.) Those Fun Runs also brought me into contact with the man who would become my running partner in long races in the future, John Lehrer. John was a writer at Runners World Magazine. Rich Benyo (one of the few people who have ever done a round trip of the Badwater Ultramarathon Run in Death Valley) was a photographer at RW. I can still see Rich hanging precariously from a tree on Moody Road to get pictures of the Fun Runners as we came charging down Moody Road to the finish.

By the end of that year my weight was down to 152 pounds, a drop of almost 70 pounds, far exceeding my expectations.

FLASHBACK: When in Rome do what the Romans do. Ditto 'flakey' California. Within six months after moving to California I started seeing an Indian guru, one Baba Muktananda, complete with an ashram in Berkeley. In my second session with Baba he gave me a mantra that I was to recite over and over to "take me to a far better place." One day I started out on a long trail run into the hills near my home. I decided to try reciting my mantra while running and see what happened. How could it hurt: meditation is good, right? So as I got into my run I silently chanted, "Om nama shivaya. Om nama shivaya." All of a sudden I found myself right running down the middle of Page Mill Road with an angry driver honking behind me. I was miles from where I had started chanting and I had absolutely no recollection of how I got there or what had happened in between. That scared the bejabbers out of me. I quit seeing the good Baba.

FLASHBACK: October, 1975. I am in Golden Gate Park, closing in on the finish of a 10 km race. For some reason I am feeling insanely good and am running strongly and easily. And fast. Today is definitely my day. There is a cool breeze coming in from the Pacific at the west end of the park. Now I can see the stadium where we will finish, so I crank up my engine, surprised at how much steam I have left, passing one fatigued runner after another. My vision narrows and all I can see is the entrance to the stadium, getting closer and closer. My legs are flying, my heart is pounding at about 180, my lungs are sucking air like a bellows, and it feels great: that's what my body is supposed to be doing. The finish line clock tells me that I have run a sub-forty minute race, something that I had never before done. I savor the moment: This day, this race, will be burned into my memory forever.

LSD RUNNING

Joe Henderson, the Editor-In-Chief of Runners World, had a theory that long, slow distance (LSD) training would be great for increasing endurance, and would be less injurious than piling on speed work on the track. A bunch of us became his LSD groupies and we ran on hilly California trails with Joe every Saturday morning. I remember pounding the trails with Lee and Winnie Jebian, Ron Kovacs and Dale Yee, moseying along at LSD pace for hours on end. The runs through the forest were tranquil, a respite from the high pressure busy-ness of go-go Silicon Valley below. Afterwards we would go out for a high-carbohydrate breakfast and talk about our run, a bunch of dirty, smelly runners sitting around and scarfing down pancakes with lots of butter and syrup. Sometimes, though, things work out a little differently.

The forested hills to the west of Silicon Valley, where we got our weekly LSD fix, are steep, rugged and bone dry most of the year. One Saturday we were on a section of scrubby deer trail that was very narrow, without a straight stretch more than ten feet long. We were running downhill on a steep section and I was in the caboose position, with Joe Henderson, Ron Kovacs and Lee and Winnie Jebian out of sight around a bend, maybe 30 yards ahead of me, when the crumbly soil beneath my feet gave way and sent me tumbling over the edge of a 40 foot drop. *Oh shit, oh shit, oh shit!* I instinctively spread-eagled my arms and legs to keep from rolling and to protect my head and face as I bounced my way down. On the way down the slope I bounced off manzanita, prickly pear cactus and rocks. By spread-eagling I had protected my head, but my bouncing body caused a mini avalanche of clods, rocks and brambles. When I hit the bottom I was covered with cuts, thorns, bruises and road rash. I lay there half buried in dirt for a couple of minutes, glad to be alive. A quick inventory indicated no broken bones, but I looked like hell and felt really bad. There was no way for my buddies to know that I had taken a dive. I didn't know exactly where I was, but I was sure that I had to get out of there fast. There were plenty of mountain lions, coyotes and rattlesnakes in the area, and I did not want to meet up with them. I knew that I had to head east to get back to civilization, and the morning sun told me which way to go.

After following the valley floor for half an hour, I saw a ranch house in the distance and heard big dogs barking. When the lady of the house spotted me headed her way, she sent her two German shepherds out to chase me off. I don't blame her: I was filthy, looked like a nut case or a vagrant wearing only shorts and sneakers, covered with dirt and blood, and I was trespassing on her property. Her dogs chased me to the top of a shed and kept me there. The woman behind the door looked scared and angry. I hope she isn't packing a shotgun. When she peeked out the cracked-open door, I shouted, *"Call 'em off lady. I'm harmless and I'm injured and I need help to get out of here".* It took a while to convince her, but eventually she called off the dogs and allowed me in to use her phone. She gave Sylvia instructions on how to get to her remote ranch, and in 15 minutes I was on my way to the emergency room at El Camino Hospital for pebble and thorn extraction and general decontamination.

Later I asked Lee Jebian if they had missed me and he said, "When we finished running I asked where you were and someone said that you had probably turned back and gone home. So we went to breakfast without you." Thanks, pals!

And they say that running is a non-contact sport.

FLASHBACK: I am running alone on a trail early in the morning, about five miles from home and about a half hour from the nearest road. On a steep downhill stretch I spot a rattlesnake sunning itself in the middle of the narrow trail a few yards ahead of me. I am going downhill too fast to stop, so I make a quick decision to jump over it instead of stepping on it. Big mistake! As my foot passes over him, he strikes up and bites me on my right Achilles tendon. It is like a burning coal and I know that I am in trouble. My mind is racing. What the hell am I going to do now? I remember two things about rattlesnake bites: first, suck the wound to get the venom out. Think about that: sucking your own Achilles tendon. Try it! I also remember that they say that if you are bitten you should sit down, relax and wait for help. I am alone in the forest far from the nearest road. Choice: sit here and die slowly or take my chances and get the hell out of here.

Down the trail I crash, right through Hidden Villa Ranch, headed for Moody Road where I might find help. I position myself in the middle of the narrow road so a passing motorist has to stop or run me over. The first car to come along is driven by a young guy who works at a local bank. When I ask him to take me to El Camino Hospital he tells me,

*"Gee, I'd like to help, but I will be late to work and I'll get in trouble."
I inform him that I am a customer at his bank, and that he will be in
much bigger trouble with his manager if he refuses to help. He opts to
accept the mantle of the good Samaritan.*

*In the emergency room I am seen by Doctor Register, who is knowl-
edgeable about snake bites after spending time in the jungles of Brazil.
He examines the bite and says, "Since it has been more than a half hour
since you were bitten, you are in little danger of dying." He offers me the
antivenin, but warns that it would be worse than the bite. "Go home
and live with it. Ice your ankle. In a few days it will go away, but in
the meantime it will be irritated and painful." For five days my ankle
is swollen, painful, hot and red. Running is not an option. I am going
nuts without getting any exercise. On Saturday I drive to San Francisco
to swim in the cold, salt water of the Bay. When I come out of the water
my ankle is back to normal. The magic of salt water!*

*The lesson here is that if you are faced with the same choice, step
on the damned snake. You might end up getting bit, but at least you
will get your revenge.*

Snakes were not the only critters in those hills. There were plenty of coyotes, bobcats, the occasional bear and no shortage of mountain lions. There were two times when I came across cougars while
running there. The first time was a chance, fleeting sighting: the cat
did not want to be seen. The second time I saw a mother and a large
cub on a mountain road about 200 yards ahead of me. They were
dragging a deer carcass into the bush, and when they spotted me they
stopped. Their eyes and ears turned menacingly in my direction. I
am no hero and I was not about to argue with them about possession
of a dead deer. I slowly backed up and proceeded in the direction
that I had come from, making sure not to look panicked, looking
back over my shoulder from time to time to make sure that I had no
company. The hairs on the back of my neck stayed bristled up for

about 20 minutes. That year, not far from Sacramento, a runner was killed by a 70 pound female with a cub.

***

SIDEBAR: RUNNING MAGAZINES IN THE SEVENTIES

In the early 1970s there were two just magazines that covered the sport of running in the United States, TRACK AND FIELD NEWS and RUNNERS WORLD. Curiously, they were located within a few miles of each other in Mountain View, California, although there was no connection between them. TRACK AND FIELD NEWS dealt with track running, with emphasis on track and field meets. The focus of RUNNERS WORLD was on road and distance running, covering road races and marathon events. If I recall correctly, TFN was largely filled with numbers and race results. RW, with Joe Henderson in the editor's seat, made an attempt to put out a more literary publication, not only with race coverage, but also interesting articles. They also published books by the then-gurus of the sport, like Joan Ullyot and George Sheehan. There was an unfortunate period when the publisher of RW (not Joe Henderson) ended up in court when he was accused of cheating his writers of their royalties. Some of us rejoiced when he sold the magazine.

My growing family in 1965. Left to right: Victoria, Sylvia (wife), Christopher, Joe and Danny

Partaking of nature's bounty, wild berries, on a long run.

Birds of a Feather

"The purpose of life, after all, is to live it, to taste experience to the utmost, to reach out eagerly and without fear for newer and richer experiences."
  – Eleanor Roosevelt

"We take care of our health, we lay aside money, we make our roof tight and our clothing sufficient, but who provides wisely in the best property of all, friends?"
  – Emerson

In Forest Park, Portland, Oregon

I feel most alive when I am moving along a forest path, the canopy of trees above me, the soft earth beneath my feet. I can't see the wildlife, but I know they are here. A nervous red squirrel makes a rustling sound in the branches overhead. A stellar jay scolds him. Tiny dew drops glisten in the filtered sunlight like diamonds on a spider web a few inches above my head, and the geometry of it draws my eyes into the center of this elaborate dining room where the patient host just sits and waits. There are so many different greens here, the cushiony darkness of the moss that blankets decaying trees that once towered overhead, now on the ground, recycling themselves to feed the next generation; The pale green of the tall ferns, some of them turning brown at the tips; The almost black green foliage of the stately Douglas firs; the patterned brown and green of the six inch slugs that seem to exist only on wet days.

On a hot summer day the trees form an umbrella to protect me from the heat. On a cool autumn day the leaf litter makes a soft carpet for my feet. When it is pouring down rain the wetness intensifies the rich, musty smells of the forest. This is a place that I love.

Portland's Forest Park is a few minutes from my home, 5,000 acres of wilderness with almost no road access. I have so many running choices here, from the 50 kilometer long Wildwood Trail to more than a dozen shorter ones, each with its own character. The north end of the park is truly wild, far from the city, one of the last temperate rain forests in North America. I have seen a herd of elk migrating through this end. The south end takes us close to Portland's population center, through the Arboretum, terminating at the Oregon Zoo. I can run different trails all summer and always be surprised at what I come upon.

Once I ran the entire 50 kilometers of the rugged, hilly Wildwood Trail, north to south. My water and food caches were stashed conveniently along the route so I could travel completely unassisted. It was a good day and I am glad I did it … Once. Another time, over a summer, I ran the trail piecemeal with my three grandchildren. It was a gift to them to learn what their bodies can do. It was a gift to me to be with them.

CHAPTER 3
THE DOLPHIN-SOUTH-END-RUNNERS (DSE)

By 1976 I was averaging over 70 miles a week and racing every weekend, sometimes both on Saturday and Sunday. I still loved the Foothill College Fun Runs, but had fallen under the spell of one of the most charismatic men I have ever met. Walt Stack, the founder and president of the San Francisco Dolphin-South-End Runners (DSE) was, as the Irish say, "An odd bird of rare plumage," a multi-dimensional man, free of pretensions, a good athlete and a thoughtful, considerate person. He was around 70 years old at the time, and every Sunday he showed up and ran with the DSE.

The DSE put on a full schedule of foot races on Sundays in San Francisco. The entry fee at other races at the time was around $15-20, but the DSE kept it at two bucks. A volunteer (often Kevin Lee) always got there early to mark the run course. There was nothing fancy, no big awards, no tee shirts, no aid stations, but there was always a starter, a couple of timers and a brightly-colored finisher's ribbon for every runner, no matter how long it took them to finish. A typical Sunday run would draw between 60 and 100 runners. Many of them were regulars, but visitors were always enthusiastically welcomed. I remember Walter telling one woman, who demurred that she was too slow to run with us, "Lady, we will wait for you to finish even if we have to time you with a calendar." And he meant it. The DSE was a pioneer in giving female runners the same opportunities as male runners. Consider that this was at the time that Jock Semple, Race Director of the Boston Marathon, was physically evicting women from his marathon course. From the very beginning the DSE awards and recognition were exactly the same for women as they were for men.

Every Sunday we ran different routes, all over the City. Running was a great way to learn the finer points of San Francisco geography.

We ran along Ocean Beach on the west side of town, or through the hills in the Potrero District further east, and most often on the long stretch of federal parkland between Fisherman's Wharf and the Golden Gate Bridge in the north. One of my favorite runs took place every New Year's Day, when we ran across the Golden Gate Bridge and back, with bottles of champagne waiting at the finish line. There was even one whacky DSE run in which we ran to the end of the Municipal Pier, jumped into the Bay, and swam back to the start. The race distances varied, too, usually between three and six miles. When you think about running and San Francisco, the image that comes to mind is steep hills. Much of our running was in fact rather vertical. But for every uphill there will always be a downhill, and that is where we could let loose our *Kamikaze Kicks*, tearing full bore down the hills, laughing at the stunned faces of automobile drivers as we ran past their cars. The key, of course, was to keep from falling.

California has always been at the forefront of social change, and San Francisco is usually ahead of the rest of the state. The DSE was true to that tradition during the 1970s 'Running Revolution,' in terms of gender, race, ability and age equality. The DSE was then and still is a good example of the best of democracy in action. I do not think that there was another running club that could boast the diversity found at any given Sunday DSE run. The DSE did another sensitive thing: they allowed slower runners to start earlier so they could finish closer to the faster runners. The club motto has always been, *"Start slowly and taper off,"* accompanied by a cartoon rendering of a happy running turtle. During the late 1970s and early 1980s the DSE was the largest running club west of the Mississippi River. It is still one of the strongest, certainly among the oldest and the best.

In those days the largest field in any running event anywhere in the world was at the annual Bay to Breakers, a 12 kilometer run across the City of San Francisco. More than 100,000 runners gathered at the start, elite runners at the front, the rest of us further back, including those dressed as clowns, in gorilla suits, and always at least a dozen streakers wearing nothing at all. The event was hosted by the local newspaper, but it was the large contingent of DSE volunteers who made it work.

After our Sunday morning DSE runs we would meet for breakfast at a local restaurant wherever we finished. It was at those breakfasts that we heard about upcoming events, caught up on gossip, and got to know each other better. I close my eyes and am sitting at a table with Len Wallach, Walt Stack, Kevin Lee, "Weatherman" Mike Pechner, Jane Colman and Rick Shea, eating pancakes and gabbing the morning away over coffee.

Walter Stack eventually reached the point where he could run no more: his age had caught up with him. At first he tried to push himself through it, but an infected foot got the best of him. When Walter Stack passed on we got the City of San Francisco to dedicate a bench to him on the Marina Green Park, facing the Bay and his former home on Alcatraz Island. After he left us, club leadership passed to Rick Shea to Len Wallach to me and eventually to Kevin Lee, but none of us could really replace Walter. The DSE has always been run entirely by volunteers, and it takes a lot of them to put on a road race every Sunday in an urban environment. That is the legacy of Walt Stack. He built a highly spirited culture into the club that will keep it going for many years to come.

ROAD RUNNERS CLUBS OF AMERICA

The DSE is a member club of the Road Runners Clubs of America. There are RRCA clubs all over the country. Among the biggest is the New York Road Runners Club, which is responsible for the enormously popular New York Marathon. When I left San Francisco and the DSE and moved to Oregon in the year 2000 I was lucky to find the Oregon Road Runners Club (ORRC), a smaller but very active and enthusiastic Road Runners club. Not only do they have a full calendar of races, but there are mid-week training sessions, including Tuesday evening runs in Beaverton. Sometimes on Tuesday evenings I show up at the runs. I will start with them, then veer off to run at my own turtle's pace. Tortoises are welcome.

Some clubs are a bit more serious about running, and in the 1970s I came across two of them in California designed to meet the needs of senior runners. The first, Northern California Seniors, catered to runners over 40 years old, and had as members some elite competitors, including Ruth Anderson, the holder of several long distance running records. Runners like to collect tee shirts, and my oldest tee is a Northern California Seniors shirt from 1974. I do not wear it often. The other club that served older athletes, Fifty-Plus Runners, was formed by ultra-distance runner Doctor Walter Bortz, who was also my family physician.

***

SIDE BAR: ABOUT WALTER STACK: TRUE OR FALSE?

If nothing else, Walter Stack was a controversial figure. In the early 1920s he was a hungry, undisciplined 15-year-old street kid in Hamtramck, Michigan. The US Army solved his hunger problem when he signed up for a four year term. He did not like it much when they sent him to the Philippines, so he just left. When his Captain finally located him in a Philippine jail (I am told that he was caught stealing food), he offered Walter a choice. If Walter would re-enlist for an additional four years, the Army would forget about his desertion. If not, he would be sent to the US Army prison at Alcatraz in California for two years, followed by a dishonorable discharge. I can see the 15 year old kid weighing it in his mind, *"Eight years in this frigging army or two in a prison in California. I'll take the two."* And he did. Walt Stack was a prisoner at the US Army prison on Alcatraz even before it became a Federal Penitentiary housing the likes of Al Capone and the Birdman . The Rock remained an Army prison until it was turned over to the Bureau of Prisons in 1934, by which time Walter was out and working as a merchant seaman.

Is it true that Walt was a Communist? Yes, he was a card carrying member of the American Communist Party for many years. Because of that, he was considered a security risk. The House Un-American Activities Committee, under Senator Joseph McCarthy, made it impossible for Walter to pursue his livelihood as a seaman. In all the years that I knew him there was never any talk of overthrowing the government: his lifelong goal was merely to achieve fairness for the working people of America. He was a respected labor leader, an athlete, a worker and a family man.

Is it true that Walter was a drinker? You bet, he loved his booze, but I never saw him drunk. He used beer as food, often having a can or two during the later parts of a marathon, and he ran a lot of marathons.

What was his daily routine? This is hard to believe. Walter would rise very early, ride his bicycle to the Dolphin Club on Fisherman's Wharf, where we were members. He would then run from the club across the Golden Gate Bridge to Sausalito and back, a distance of 17 miles. After a swim in San Francisco Bay, he would have breakfast and ride his bike home. Then he would be at work by eight AM and work as a mason's hod-carrier, lugging bricks and mortar up a ladder on construction jobs all day long.

Is it true that he held the record for being 'bleeped' for off color language on the Johnny Carson show? Yes. In fact he set records on three different episodes of the Johnny Carson show, each time garnering more bleeps than previously. Carson loved it and encouraged him by asking leading questions. Walter had a rather salty tongue and he did little to modify his speech to satisfy someone else's sensibilities.

Is it true that he completed both the IRONMAN TRIATHLON and the WESTERN STATES 100 MILE RUN? He did complete both of those extremely long endurance events in his seventies. First was the WS 100, which he ran in 1978. I was with him in 1982 when he did the IRONMAN in Kona, Hawaii. Walt was no speed demon and by the time he finished the IRONMAN course and the aid stations were long shut down. No problem: a friend on a bicycle followed alongside him during the final 26 mile running leg, supplying Walt with beer from a cooler on the bike. At the awards ceremony the next day a polite and kindly Japanese doctor, also an elderly competitor, came to our table to ask Walter about his IRON-MAN experience. Walt told him that he was okay once he got out of the hospital. *"Why were you in the hospital, Mr. Stack?"* *"Because they had to pull that damned bicycle seat out of my ass."* The doctor paused to consider that before grinning. That was pure Walt Stack.

FLASHBACK: It is early on a Friday morning, an unusual time for me to be running in San Francisco. I am running across the Golden Gate Bridge with Walter on his daily round trip. There is no hurry. Today's fog is ten stories above us, flowing around and past the tops of the bridge towers, heading east towards Berkeley, making it difficult for the struggling sunrise to make a dent in the morning chill. Walter is bare-chested, as usual, exposing his faded tattoos. He looks like he should have a cigar hanging from his mouth. The morning commuters honk their "good mornings" at him as they drive into The City. Everybody knows Walt Stack. On the way down into Sausalito I tell him that he should run for mayor. He responds, "Maybe, but I don't think that I could handle the daily ration of bullshit and crooks. I'd rather carry my 50 pound hod."

Walt was a regular at the Pike's Peak Marathon, which starts at the cog railway at 7,000 feet and goes clear up to the top of Pike's Peak at over 14,000 feet, then down again, trashing your knees on granite all the way. He was the founder of the Peak Busters, a group that encourages women to challenge that extremely arduous event and others.

THE HASH HOUSE HARRIERS.

I don't know if the "Hash" should really be called a running club. They are truer to their professed identity as "a drinking club with a running problem." The Hash came into existence when a group of ex-pat engineers and businessmen got together in a steamy Southeast Asian British colony that was then known as Malaya (now Malaysia) in 1938. Every week they would go for a run in the jungle then meet later for food and drinks in a local dive that they called the "Hash House." The Japanese invaded Malaya shortly afterwards and the Brits either went packing home or were imprisoned. Some were sent to build "The Bridge on the River Kwai."

But stiff-upper-lip Brits will not be deterred. After the war the Hashers returned to Malaya, dug up what was left of their buried stash of drinking mugs, etc. and the Hash House Harriers was born again. (For the uninitiated, a *harrier* is a runner, and a *hash house* is a restaurant.) There are many 'hashes', as local groups are known, throughout the world, but the Mother Hash remains in beautiful Kuala Lumpur, Malaysia.

Flash forward to 1988. We are in Kuala Lumpur, the capital of what is now independent Malaysia, to celebrate the 50th anniversary of the Hash, an event called an Interhash. There are probably 5,000 Hashers here, and we will be concentrating on drinking beer and occasionally going for a semi-organized run through the rice paddies and jungles outside of KL. Keep in mind that Malaysia is a Muslim country, and alcohol is generally frowned upon. That doesn't seem to be a problem, though, because the authorities have allowed us the use of the prestigious Selangor Turf Club as our headquarters. Hashers have come here from all over Asia, Africa, North and South America, Europe and Australia. There is a large contingent of New Zealanders, who claim to be especially skilled at downing brews. We will see a Kiwi named Mongo compete against a famed Englishman in a down-down contest, in which they will race to chug a full pitcher of beer, draining it in about 15 seconds. (Let me describe Mongo: he is large of gut and walks around wearing two bandoleers of beer cans. I have never seen him without a beer in his hands.) Spillage is not allowed in a down-down contest. Rules say that it okay to puke, but it has to go into the pitcher, and you still have to down the whole damned thing. Mongo was the winner in 14 seconds, but the real hero was another Kiwi lad named Spacey, who drank, up-chucked, and finished it all in 18 seconds, winning everyone's heart. What a guy! The revelry at a big Interhash event rivals that of the New Orleans Mardi Gras and would even raise an eyebrow or two in normally nonplussed San Francisco. To tell the truth, I am sure that I had a great time at Interhash, but much of it was through a haze.

FLASHBACK: Kuala Lumpur, Maylasia, 1988. I am on a high-way in a moving bus full of Hashers, mostly Kiwis and Aussies, headed back into town after a Hash run through rice paddies in the nearby countryside. One of the shit-faced Kiwis opens a window and climbs out while two others dangle him by his ankles. The terrified Muslim driver is having a fit. For a few minutes the Kiwi makes weird gestures to passing drivers until his mates spot a cop and drag him back into the bus. In the back of the bus a Hasher from Cairo has been trying to cozy up to an intoxicated Australian girl. He finally convinces her to sit on his lap. Suddenly his eyes bulge and he shouts, "The bitch pissed on my lap!" I will probably not tell Sylvia about this bus trip.

How is it that there have come to be some 250,000 Hashers worldwide? Well, the Hash has had a long time to grow, for one thing. Over the years the main vector for spreading this disease has been through lonely ex-pat businessmen, embassy and military personnel stationed overseas. But no one can tell you for sure just how many Hashers there are, because there is no such thing as membership. There is nothing to join: You just show up when you hear about a Hash run. *For example: There are several Hash groups in the San Francisco area, and each has a hotline with info on where and when the next run will take place. There is a regular Monday evening Hash in San Francisco, and a Saturday Hash in the South Bay and another on Sunday in the Oakland area. Just call the hotline (or website http:// www.sfh3.com/) and bring a few bucks for beer money.)* You show up, you toss in your beer money, you run and you party. What could be simpler? After showing up for a few weeks, someone will get the bright idea to give you a Hash name. It will not be something that you will like, but get used to it, because the more you protest, the more you will be teased about it.

What is a typical Hash run like? There is no such thing as a typical Hash run. However, in most cases a predetermined Hare (or two of them) will be sent out 15 minutes early to set a secret course. He marks his trail with chalk or flour, leaving his marks on the ground, sidewalks, walls, etc. The Hare is required to lay out a decent course that the Hounds can follow with some difficulty. He will try to trick the Hounds with a few detours and false trails to slow down the FRBs (Front Running Bastards). I have participated in Hash runs that went through places like a Neiman-Marcus store or the Stanford campus, but they are mostly on city streets or in parks. One of my most interesting Hash runs was put on by the Hong Kong Hash House Harriers, running right along the Chinese Communist border when Hong Kong was still under British control. We ran at night with flashlights. I can still hear the Chinese border guards shouting wildly at us in the dark, but who speaks Chinese, anyway? Running through mud (shiggy) is an almost sacred a part of the game, as are places where one would normally not venture even in the daylight. Speed is not rewarded, and front runners may have to chug a 'down-down,' a pint of beer for excessive zeal. About halfway through a Hash run the Hare will provide a beer-check, a car parked by the side of the road with the trunk open and a beer keg tapped and mugs at the ready.

When the Hounds arrive at the finish, usually on the street corner where they started, there will be another keg, a lot of singing and frivolity, and the chugging of more down-downs for any reason whatsoever. Upset neighbors often call the police to have us removed. When (and if) they finally arrive, the cops will usually laugh it off and ask us politely to leave. There are, in fact, several Hashers who are police in real life, and I know of at least two judges. Then we all go to a low-end restaurant/gin mill where there will be more singing, frivolity, eating and drinking. At first the proprietors will welcome us. The younger Hashers, an undisciplined lot, might engage in a spontaneous food fight. Many restaurants come to the conclusion that they can do without the Hash's business. For several years I was afforded the dubious distinction of *songmeister* of the San Francisco Hash. After a few beers you may ask me for my bawdy version of *Frere Jacques,* but you will have to supply the virgin.

FLASHBACK: Moscow, USSR, 1984, Sunday morning. I am running in Sokolniki Park with the Moscow Hash, about 35 of us, mostly embassy employees: Brits, Yanks, Kiwis and Australians. There is one stoic Finn, an athletic looking Dane and a confused and giddy Greek. We have no permit for a gathering, a very big no-no in the highly regimented USSR, but the cops will not mess with embassy personnel because of diplomatic immunity. The locals strolling in the park do not know what to make of us: frolicking and having fun in public is very unusual in the USSR. One of the Kiwis is wearing a red tee shirt with a picture of Mickey Mouse. The evil-looking, grinning Mickey Mouse has his nasty middle finger extended upward, balancing the Red Star. After the run we go to the New Zealand embassy for our post-Hash party, with free-flowing beer and vodka and a lot of singing. The guy sitting next to me is a US Marine sergeant, an embassy guard. A year of so later I read that he has been arrested for bringing his Russian girlfriend and her "uncle" into the restricted code room at the embassy.

If you are interested in debasing yourself by running with a local Hash group, start by asking around at a nearby running store. They might claim ignorance, so try the Internet under Hash House Harriers. You will eventually find them under a rock someplace. Bring your sense of humor and be ready for the unexpected. Don't wear your Sunday best clothing. If you are not a beer drinker and a rabble rouser, don't waste your time with the Hash.

Flashback: Golden Gate Park, San Francisco, Monday evening. The Hares this evening are Norman "Cumming Mutha" Wheatley and his beautiful and intelligent wife, "On-All-Fours." Norman is a wild Australian, so you never know what he is going to do next. Tonight's twilight Hash run takes us into Golden Gate Park, not an unusual venue for the SF Hash. Norman has a different twist on this one. The beer check is three miles into the run, at the halfway point, but there is no beer keg. Instead he has brewed up a big pot of a witch's brew of hard liquor and fruit juice. Just what I need during a six mile run! I take one drink and it tastes good. I linger and imbibe a second and a third. Why not? Now I feel like Superman, but unlike Superman I can't really fly. Someone should have told me that before I started down that steep, rugged hill. Down the hill I zoom, not paying attention to the reality of gravity. I end up at the bottom in a crumpled ball of me. I get up laughing and try to run. My left ankle hurts like heck and I feel blood running down my cheek. Two kindly Hashers help me to my car, a stick shift, which I have to drive 40 miles to El Camino Hospital to get

35

patched up.   Moral: Don't drink and try to fly.

(For the curious, my Hash name is "F'n Nuts". That came about at a San Francisco Monday evening run when a Hasher asked, "Where is Oakes." The response was that I was crossing Siberia on foot, to which he responded, "He must be f**king nuts. There was general agreement on that count, and I was baptized accordingly at my next hash run.)

Walt Stack's 85th birth-day party, after a DSE run, 1992.

Walt Stack was my mentor. Note out turtle mascot. Our club motto is START SLOWLY AND TAPER OFF. Good advice anytime.

My 60th birthday in 1994 with the SF Hash House Harriers. Note how nicely they treated me. My birthday cake was smashed in my face and I had to chug a beer from my smelly running shoe.

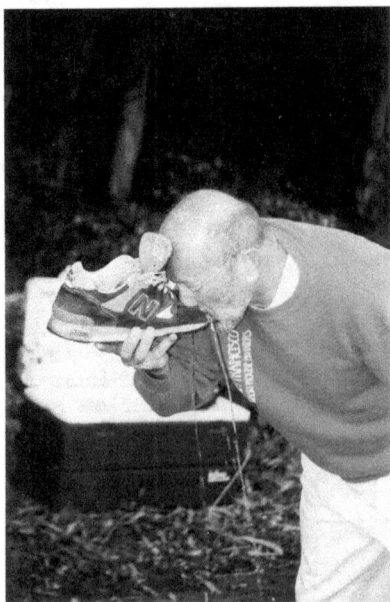

The Miracle of the Marathon: It's Good to be the King

"I believe man will not merely endure, he will prevail. He is immortal, not because he, alone among creatures, has an inexhaustible voice but because he has a ... spirit capable of compassion and sacrifice and endurance."
— *William Faulkner*

"Victory belongs to the most persevering."
— *Napoleon*

"A ship is safe in harbor, but that's not what ships are for."
— *William Shedd*

How many times have you heard someone say, "Someday I am going to run a marathon?" How many of them eventually run one? Quite a few, actually. Witness the thousands who show up at the starting lines of the New York, London, Chicago or Los Angeles marathons. There is a magical draw to that mythical distance. Completing a marathon is a heroic feat, an accomplishment that both elevates you into rarified company and at the same time binds you to the classical Greek runner, Phidippides, the original marathon runner. Once you have run a marathon, you have become a new person. It is like attaining the rank of Eagle Scout: when you have earned that coveted badge, it can never be taken away from you. You are forever a marathoner.

But first, you have to actually get off the couch and run that marathon. I do not promise that it will be easy.

CHAPTER 4
IT'S GOOD TO BE THE KING

The term 'marathon' refers to something very specific in the world of running. To be certified as a marathon, a course must be measured by a trained specialist, and it must be precisely 26 miles, 385 yards, within extremely narrow tolerances. That is the distance of the Olympic Marathon, the New York Marathon, Boston, and it is the same for all modern proper marathon races. The word 'marathon' dates back to the war between ancient Greece and Persia. A runner named Phidippides ran the entire distance from the battlefield on the Plains of Marathon to Athens to bring news to his countrymen about their victory over the Persians. Legend says that Phidippides died of exhaustion after he delivered the news. No one today knows exactly where he started or where he finished, or even if he actually died because of his effort. But when the first modern Olympic Games took place in Greece in 1896 the authorities settled on 25 miles as a fair estimate of how far he actually ran. That was good enough until, a couple of Olympiads later in England, the distance was changed so the race would finish where the King had decided to sit to observe the finish of the marathon. True? Beats me, but it is as good a reason for an unreasonable change as any. Wasn't 25 miles a nice enough round number? But everyone knows that the King of England can plunk his royal butt wherever it pleases him. To quote Mel Brooks, "It's good to be the King."

For the mathematically inclined among us, think about how many footsteps it would take to run a marathon. A mile is 5280 feet long, and a marathon is more than 26 times that distance. If your stride length is five feet you will take more than 1,000 steps per mile. That means that in a marathon your feet will strike the ground n excess of 26,000 times. Most marathon runners do not take five foot long strides, so the number of foot strikes is more like 30,000 impacts. Is it any wonder that almost all distance runners develop foot, ankle, hip, back and/or knee problems?

I have run 130 standard distance marathons in all, including at least one on every continent. Some of them were great fun, some were quite difficult. I would like to tell you about a few of those that were most meaningful to me. (If 130 sounds like a lot, there are runners who have run many more than that. Sy Mah, Toledo, ran over 600 before passing away. Greg Brown of the DSE is currently over 300.)

My first attempt at the distance, the San Mateo Marathon, featured an industrial area in California, and was organized by an entrepreneur named Jack Leydig. It was a hot day, the course ran along smelly Hwy 101, an ugly, lousy course and the truth be told, I was far from ready for any marathon: I had simply not done enough preparation. I may be short on brains, but have never been short of balls. I had devised an elaborate plan of exactly how many minutes and seconds each mile would take me. The plan was a pipe dream, wishful thinking, and it lasted just one mile. When I finally finished my marathon I was a basket case, puking on myself and anything nearby, writhing in agony on the ground, a very unhappy and disillusioned man. My 14 year old son Dan had accompanied me to the race. If he laughed he was dead meat. I think my misery that day cured him of ever wanting to be a distance runner. Dan did not yet have a driver's license, but that did not stop me from pleading with him to drive the car carrying my failed and agonized body home. I puked again in the bathtub at home. In my agony I swore an oath that I would never attempt to run another marathon.

The Japanese have a saying: *"A man who has never climbed Mount Fuji is a fool. A man who climbs it twice is a bigger fool."* Sure as shooting, I signed on for my next marathon as soon as I had my memory lapse. But this time I really trained hard. During that period I averaged over 60 miles a week, including speed work on the Foothill College track, fartlek, and a lot of long, slow distance (LSD) running. My preparation took six months, and when I toed the line at the Avenue of the Giants Marathon in Weott, California, I was ready. Here is what that course is like: You run along a road in the Redwoods National Forest. The road is lined on both sides by enormous redwood trees hiding the sky. It is L-shaped, out-and-back, starting and finishing at the L juncture. The trees provide shade, and there is a light mist off the Pacific in the air. For a marathon runner, cool is golden. Put that together with the magnificent scenery and the fact that the course is mostly flat, and you have the formula for success. I ran well that day and enjoyed every minute of it. I even had enough left at the finish to race a 13 year old girl the final 200 yards. (Her kick was better than mine.) I highly recommend the Avenue of the Giants for a first or a fiftieth marathon. Considering my lack of experience, I was satisfied with myself that day, finishing under three and a half hours. In my mind I had become a marathoner.

FLASHBACK: I am at mile 22 in the 1975 Avenue of the Giants Marathon. Gigantic skyscraper-high redwood trees tower above the runners, forming an overhead cathedral arch to shelter us in a cool, almost spiritual atmosphere. When I breathe, tiny droplets of fog deliciously moisten my tongue and throat. To my right I see where a black bear has left his claw marks on a tree trunk. I slow down at the aid station and take in two full Dixie cups of delicious water, deciding that this will be my last water stop before the finish: at this pace I have just over a half hour more to go. I'm feeling confident about finishing but, as Yogi Berra said, "It ain't over 'til it's over." I do a quick self inventory: Feel pretty good mentally; right knee bitching just a little; feet hot and wet, but not bad; I have been drinking enough, and had an energy drink at mile 20. From this point on, I think that I will make it to my first decent marathon finish.

I was determined to learn the craft of running, and what better source than other runners. They were very helpful in getting me to the point where I could run my races more comfortably and competently. For example, John McCrillis, a co-worker and a fine runner, offered this little tip: Before leaving the house, drink two cups of hot water; that way you will have your 'movement' before leaving the house and avoid the long lines of the smelly Port-a-Potties. Little things, as they say, mean a lot.

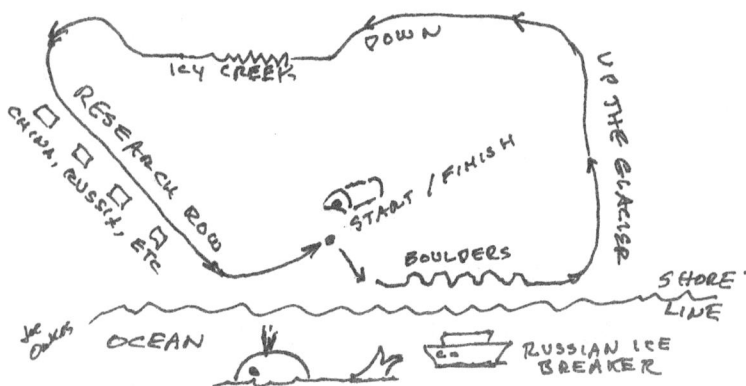

Antarctica Marathon

ANTARCTICA

With so many marathons to look back on, it is hard to select a favorite. The most interesting one was called The Last Marathon, held in Antarctica on February 5, 1995. A travel company called Marathon Tours and Travel (MTT) in Boston takes runners to marathons all over the world. The owner, a guy named Gilligan, had the very creative idea to produce a marathon in Antarctica, something that had never been done before. Why had it never been done? First, it is really, really far away from anyplace else, so getting people there would be no easy chore. Second, the logistics of putting on a marathon in a roadless area and in a very hostile environment presents some extremely huge problems. MMT recruited the assistance of the various international research stations working on the Antarctic Peninsula. Their second wonderful idea was to hire a Russian ice-breaker to transport the runners to the frozen continent. The bills would be high. In order to make it happen, they would have to charge quite a bit more than the going rate for a marathon. They put the word out in the trade publications, Runners World et al. Their call-to-arms succeeded to the point that they had to hire a second Russian ice breaker to transport about 85 runners and companions.

We boarded the Russian ships in Ushuaia, Argentina, the southernmost city in the world. From there the crossing of tumultuous Drake's Passage involved a brutal 40 hours of massive waves crashing over the deck. Most of the runners came down with bad cases of seasickness. But our little Akademik Ioffe was up to the task and we eventually reached the less stormy waters to the west of the Antarctic Peninsula. Nobody goes to Antarctica just to run a marathon. Our hosts arranged for the ship's zodiacs to take us ashore in several interesting places. On our shore excursions and at sea we saw many penguins (adelies, chinstraps, magellanic), Wedell seals, elephant seals, fur seals, leopard seals, killer whales, minke whales, right whales, blue whales and dolphins, some of them very close. For me the best part of the preliminary activities was having the ship sail into the sunken caldera of volcanic Deception Island. What a wonderful and seemingly incongruous combination: snow on the flanks of the volcano and hot fumeroles bubbling up sulfurous steam in the icy water-filled crater. Peter Butler, Bruce Horowitz, Ben Jones, Joe Womersley and I went ashore in the zodiac to do some skinny dipping in the crater. Our guide for the swim was the ship's Russian medical officer, a chubby, grandmotherly woman. She knew every inch of the crater, and she and I swam about a mile in the caldera, carefully navigating between the hot, smelly, bubbling fumaroles and the icy drainage from the slopes. It was one of the best and weirdest swim adventures of my entire life.

On marathon day the Russian captain anchored the ship a quarter mile off Research Row, where Russia, China and several other nations maintain 'research' stations. (While I do not doubt that some legitimate research does take place, 'research' seems to be a euphemism for maintaining a landed presence so when the Antarctic Treaty finally falls apart those countries will have feet on the ground for long-awaited mineral exploitation.) Because the near-shore water was too shallow for the Russian ships, we went ashore in the 'rubber duckie' zodiacs. Our hosts were the scientists at the Chilean station, and that is where our marathon would start and finish. Their station was a big quonset hut where the lonely scientists lived and worked. Our hosts were overjoyed to have us visit; they do not get many visitors in the Antarctic.

When it was time for us to run, Gilligan explained that the marathon course would consist of two loops, each a half-marathon, 13.1 miles. We would first run across a boulder field by the shore, then straight up the face of a glacier, and make a left turn down its steep left flank. After that we would be running in a snow-melt creek bed that would lead us to the gravel road that connects all the research stations, and on back to our starting point. After that we would continue on to run our second 13.1 mile loop. Since there were no trails most of the way, the organizer had jammed six-inch wires with red flags into the ice along the route. The only aid stations would be at the various research stations.

We had come to the 'frigid' Antarctic expecting very cold temperatures, and had brought clothing that was appropriate for a cold climate. Instead the temperature was a few degrees above freezing:

tropical for that part of the world. The high temperatures, the result of global warming, had in fact melted the snow that had covered the boulder field for centuries. Melting snow had also created the creek bed that we had to run in. Still, knowing that we had to traverse a glacier, most of us were cautious and dressed warmly. The first part of the run was brutal and very slow: a quarter of a mile of ankle breaking boulders the size of microwaves and washing machines before we could start our climb up the glacier. It was more clambering than running, sometimes doubled over. The glacier itself was not especially steep, but going up it was slippery and we had to be very watchful to avoid crevasses hidden under the snow. I had sunk several screws into the soles of my running shoes for added traction. The red flags that had been placed to mark the route were stolen by big voracious birds called skuas, so we had to go by dead reckoning. Skuas will eat or steal anything, especially baby penguins. Up the glacier we went, over a mile up, fortunately losing no one into a crevasse. Down its left flank we ran and slid until we came to the creek bed. We were expecting to find a nice, smooth creek bed to run in. Instead it was deep, oozing mud, much to the chagrin of Peter Butler, who lost a shoe 16 inches into the mud. On his hands and knees in the icy water, he groped in the mud until he was able to yank it free against the suction. Then he had to wash the mud out and put it back on.

FLASHBACK: I am afraid that Peter Butler is pissed at me because I am roaring with laughter as he gets down on his hands and knees to dig in the icy mud for his shoe. He glares at me, then breaks out laughing himself and tosses a handful of frigid mud at me, which I decide that I will wear for the rest of the race as a badge of honor. There can be absolutely nothing serious about this marathon: we are here to have a great Antarctic experience so who gives a damn if we finish in three hours or ten?

We were wet, cold and filthy when we came to the first of the aid stations, at the Great Wall Research Station, manned by formal Chinese scientists, who seem a bit concerned about muddy-buddies Peter and Joe. As we approached they greeted us with solemnity as they offered us cups of sweet tea. These gentle men had never experienced marathon runners before and had never met an American. I am sure that they are still talking about us back home in China. On we ran, our next stop the station run by Russian scientists. More tea? *"Nyet! Vodka much better for runner. More energy, and you no feel pain."* We continued in this surrealistic atmosphere, research station after research station, down the road returning to our starting point. Here we shed excess clothing, lots of it. By this time we had already run a half marathon and many of the runners decided that they had had enough of Antarctic marathoning. The rest of us continued on, across the boulder field again, up and down the glacier, through the muddy creek and down the road manned by incredulous scientists.

Those of us who finished became the first runners to ever have run a marathon in the Antarctic, for what that's worth, and I have a tee shirt to show for it. It was an experience that I truly loved.

MARABANA

(If I admit to going to Cuba to run a marathon, then I might be admitting to breaking US law. No way! So read this, if you will, as if it is a bit of fantasy. Or not.)

In 1997 six of us flew to Toronto so we could catch a plane to Havana. What a pain in the ass. We had to go that roundabout route for two reasons. First, there were no flights from the US to our dreaded evil nemesis, Cuba. Second, our government had us believing that it would be illegal for us to go there. (The fact is that *going* to Cuba was not illegal: *spending money* there was, assuming that you got caught.) The officials at Cuban immigration understood the problem that American citizens had, so they did not stamp our passports, helping us to keep our deep, dark secret. About 100,000 Americans per year are not fooled or bullied by the US government: they go to Cuba regardless of the so-called rules and misinformation. Think about that, Washington, DC bureaucrats!

Our first stop was at the modern, luxurious Hotel Cuatro Palmas in Varadero Beach, several miles from Havana. It came as a bit of enlightenment that there were guests in the tourist area of Varadero Beach from all over Europe, and that several European countries had direct flights to Havana. Hmmm! *Europeans* were enjoying the magnificent beaches, the great music, the culture of Cuba, and the investment opportunities while Americans, just 75 miles away, had hamstrung ourselves from the game because some people in Washington did not like a guy named Fidel Castro. (Fidel eventually outlasted eight US presidents.) What the hell, I was not going to be deterred by outdated politics: there was a fine, white sand beach just outside my bedroom. So I swam in the glorious, warm and soothing sea to wash away my sins and cleanse my soul, a baptism of sorts. *Mea culpa.* Screw the stupid rules.

The marathon, *Marabana* (a contraction of marathon-habana) was coming up, so we relocated to downtown Havana, where the run would start just opposite the national capital, an identical copy of our national capitol. We were put up at the formerly elegant Hotel Sevilla. If you are a student of history you might recall that the Hotel Sevilla was the headquarters of the US Mafia during the time when the Cuban government was run by a combination of American mafiosi and a very corrupt and cooperative Presidente Fulgencio Batista. (Fidel Castro sent the Mafia and Batista packing, but he was a dirty, stinking Commie, so we could not be buddies.) Regular US mob guests at the Sevilla were Santos Trafficante, boss of the Tampa, Florida branch of the Mafia, and Chicago's Al Capone, who retained the entire eighth floor for his cronies. The guest list also included luminaries like Joe Louis, Ted Williams, Enrico Caruso and a host of major US politicians. We were in good company at the Sevilla, even if they were only ghosts.

But we were in Cuba to run, not to hobnob with dead Mafiosi. Registration was easy: you just went to a building across from the Cuban capitol and paid your five dollar entry fee. (Of course we did not actually spend money in Cuba, right?) There were about 3,000 runners, some of them from Germany, France, Italy, Canada and Caribbean islands. Marathon day arrived and we were ready. So was Jupiter Pluvius, the god of torrential rain. I have run in all kinds of weather, but the rain that fell that day was the worst I have ever seen. It caused rivers to flow in the streets. No matter, the run must go on, and for the thousands of Cuban runners, rain did not seem to be a problem. But it made for a very slow and soaking wet, if warm, marathon. I can close my eyes and see Janet Rensch and John Lang, two of our team, coming across the finish line, looking like drowned rats, beaming as happy as can be. I can also see dozens of Cuban runners running the entire course bare foot simply because they did not own running shoes. When our group returned home we gave our used shoes to local runners: those used shoes were the best shoes they ever had. We also left a carton of shoes donated by our running friends back home in San Francisco.

FLASHBACK: Walking around in the Marabana finish area is a pretty teenager, maybe 16 years old, draped in the remnants of an American flag, cut bikini-style. Clearly she is not a runner. She approaches our American group, gives a big, suggestive, sexy smile and says that she wants to go to America. "Maybe you know someone who is looking for a beautiful wife? I speak English good and I can cook." She is younger than my oldest granddaughter.

FLASHBACK: Mile two of the 1978 Boston Marathon. We are not far from the start in Hopkinton, still 24 miles from the downtown finish. From here I can see the jumble of the city's skyline far away in the distance. All of a sudden it occurs to me that, I am actually going to run all the way there. Wow! I realize that if I can see something far away in the distance, I can actually use my feet to take me there. That is a powerful feeling!

Memories, images keep popping up. It is Patriot's Day, April 1978, and I am sprinting towards the finish line of the Boston Marathon. Over 1,000 runners have finished ahead of me and more thousands are behind me. There are thousands of cheering spectators behind the police barricades on both sides of the road. As I make the final sharp turn, I trip and fall to the ground, just yards from the finish. I sit dazed on the ground. A well-meaning bystander ducks under the police barrier to help me to my feet, when a rotund Boston cop intercedes: "Don' touch 'im. He will get disquawlified." I get to my feet and chuckle as I run the last few yards.

The next year I ran the New York Marathon; I can still see the dignified Hasidic Jews in Brooklyn with their black felt hats, long black overcoats and side curls, and the giggling black kids as we pass through Harlem, reveling in spraying the runners with hoses. That day we ran in all five boroughs and across five bridges. As we passed through the Bronx the course took us in front of the 40th Precinct police station where many years before, as a teenager, I spent some unhappy hours.

Marathon runners are always trying ways to improve our chances of getting past 'the Wall' that descends upon us in the late stages of a marathon. There was the time during the San Francisco Mayor's Cup Marathon that I got a little too scientific and decided that a good experimental energy replacement drink might be orange juice and vodka. I had a bottle of the stuff stashed in the bushes at the 20-mile mark. Walt Stack used beer for energy, so I figured that if Walt Stack could drink beer during a run, then vodka might be an even better way to avoid 'the wall'. It's basic chemistry: burning alcohol produces a lot of energy. I finished, but the result was not what I anticipated. My gut was in rebellion and I was miserably sick. I ended up vomiting very loudly, right behind the flatbed trailer where Mayor Mosconi was making a speech congratulating the finishers. My loud barfing was amplified over his microphone for all to hear. (Not long after Mayor Mosconi, a decent and forward-looking man, was murdered by a demented rival politician.)

MONTREAL

Some memories flow in more vividly than others. The Montreal Marathon started on the Jacques Cartier Bridge above the Saint Lawrence River. Hundreds of runners were lined up on the bridge, far above the boat traffic passing below us. The organizers gave us a three minute warning and a great cheer went out from the crowd. I asked the fellow next to me, "What is that all about?" He replied, "Look around you and you will see." Hundreds of runners were urinating off the bridge, some of them squatting, some peeing over the rail. "It is our tradition." When in Rome, do as the Romans. I suggest that you try not to be under the bridge at the start of the Montreal Marathon.

I enjoyed running that marathon with a close Canadian friend. The course was not terribly difficult. Like the New York Marathon it took us through neighborhoods that most visitors would probably have no reason to visit. All along the way the dynamism of the people burst forth, grandmothers shouting from windows, *"Allez, allez! Champeon! Allez!"* They were really into it; it made the marathon much more pleasant. Here is another picture from Montreal: As we passed through an industrial area, I was told that we would observe another tradition just ahead. In a vacant lot dozens of runners were facing a wall, emptying their bladders. "That is our version of hitting the wall." Afterwards we went out for breakfast at Beauty's, famous for its bagels. The after-run camaraderie is one of the best parts of running, especially when you are hungry and have something to rejoice.

HELSINKI

Decades before the Ethiopian and Kenyan runners came to dominance in distance running, Finland reigned supreme, starting with the Paavo Nurmi, the Flying Finn. I was in Helsinki to run the marathon. What a thrill it was to be competing there, a place where distance running is the national sport! But the Finnish people are a dour lot, and along the entire course there was not a cheer to be heard, no one shouting encouragement for the runners. Perhaps they could benefit from a visit by a group of cheering grandmothers from Montreal. I do have two good memories of running in Helsinki. First, outside the Olympic Stadium is a statue of the demi-god of running, Paavo Nurmi in full flight. It is a large bronze with the Flying Finn precariously balanced on one toe. At the finish, when entering the stadium, I was amazed to see myself displayed on a gigantic video screen on the other side of the field.

LIVERMORE, CA

Of all my marathons, one still bothers me. There was a time when, because I could maintain a very steady pace, I was sometimes asked to pace people who wanted to finish in a specific time. That happened at the Livermore Marathon when a female runner had arranged for me to pace her at eight minutes per mile for the first half marathon, after which she would retire from the run. When she left the course we were about 90 seconds ahead of schedule and she was happy. An eight minute per mile pace comes quite close to three and a half hours for a full marathon, and my goal for the day was to finish in 3:27-3:29, which seemed reasonable. I was already halfway there and feeling strong. Two miles later the course passed through a school yard. A fellow in front of me had stopped running. He seemed to be having a bad time, and as I went by, I tapped his elbow to encourage him. He picked up his pace and joined me. As we ran together he told me that his goal was to make the 3:30 cutoff that was the qualifying time for 40 year olds for the Boston Marathon. When I told him that I would be finishing in slightly under 3:30 he said the he would like to tag along. He seemed to be doing well, so when we reached mile 25 I picked up my pace and left him to finish the last mile honorably on his own. My finish time was 3:28:30. He never finished. I started jogging back along the course and was shocked to see the medics loading him into an ambulance: he had died, not a quarter mile from the finish. I did not know the man, but when I later located and called to his wife, she explained that he knew that he had a serious heart condition and that his doctor had advised against running a marathon. At that point I made the decision that I would never push another runner, and I would never pace a runner I did not know really well.

So many miles, so many marathon, so many memories! I ran enough marathons that, if linked together end to end, they would take me all the way across the United States. My fastest time? For a while I tried to get under three hours. I came very close several times before deciding that it was not much fun being in agony at the finish line. It occurred to me that if I ran each mile of the marathon just a few seconds slower, I could stay within my comfort zone. My overall time might be a few minutes slower, but I would enjoy my run more and feel much better after finishing. I would also recover much more quickly and be able to run again sooner. Screw Phidipides and dropping dead at the finish line! There are more important things in life.

A word about setting time goals for a marathon: Unless you are a top competitive runner, I do not recommend setting very specific finishing time goals under any circumstances. Here is why. My friend Bill was a pretty good runner, but he got it into his head that he *absolutely* had to break three hours for a marathon. It was as though his life depended on it and little else mattered to him. He had already run three marathons between 3:04 and 3:10 and was frustrated. Bill hired a good coach, trained really hard, and paid his coach to pace him for his crowning effort. They stayed together like Siamese twins for the entire distance, coach a step ahead, drafting for him. They were running right at a three hour pace. At mile 23 the coach gave Bill a pill: God knows what it was: it was either something illegal or a placebo. As they reached the finish line, his coach literally shoved Bill across the line. He finished in 2:59:59. Bill finally had done his sub-three marathon, but he soon lost interest and quit running for good. What was wrong with Bill's obsession? For one thing, he got his head tangled up between two completely arbitrary numbers that had nothing to do with him or his running ability. First, the distance was the result of where the king of England had planted his royal butt, and that had nothing to do with Bill. Second, setting a time of three hours was not a function of Bill's innate ability, just a round number on the clock. What would be wrong with feeling good about running a good race, maybe your best race, regardless of what the clock says? (I don't think anyone was timing Phidipides in ancient Greece.) Why not run because you love it, not because you are knotted up at the intersection of a pair of irrelevant numbers? I miss running with my friend Bill. But his wife is happy because he is home all the time now instead of "wasting his time running around in circles with those other idiots."

GETTING TO THE STARTING LINE

This isn't about running an actual marathon, it is about how we got to the starting line of a marathon. Several years ago a friend and I signed up to run the Wild, Wild West Marathon, which is held in the late spring on the desert (east) side of the Sierra Nevada Mountains, not far north of the town of Lone Pine, California. But we lived on the San Francisco peninsula, which is on the west side of the Sierras.

Here is the problem we were faced with: Because it was early in the season, none of the mountain passes across the Sierra Nevada were open: they were still snowed in. We talked about it. To get to the start, we would have to drive a roundabout route via Los Angeles to the south, a very long detour. George (he asked me not to use his real name) suggested that we did not have to take the detour: we could just leave a day early and run across the mountains to get to the east side, then run the Wild, Wild West Marathon the next day. That worried me a little. "George, if all the roads are still snowed in, won't there be plenty of snow in the mountains? And the shortest route is about 35 miles." George agreed with the distance, but convinced me that the snow would probably not be very deep, and it might be a great adventure. "And what is the big deal about hiking 35 miles?"

George and I were both dumb enough to think that we could pull it off and it might really be fun. We had a friend drop us off at 0600 east of Fresno inside the Big Trees entrance to Sequoia National Park. After dropping us off, Marty, our driver would continue south, loop around the mountains and meet us at around five that evening in a place called Onion Valley above Bishop, California. Eleven hours should be plenty of time for us to hike 35 miles.

We wore lightweight wind breakers, long sleeved tee shirts, wool hats, long Gore Tex exercise pants and gloves. We had to travel light, carrying only the high energy food that could fit into the pockets of our jackets and an empty water bottle. For water we would eat snow. On our feet we wore ordinary running shoes over wool socks, and we each carried an extra pair of socks in our pockets. To keep the weight down we would decided not to carry flashlights, backpacks, a stove or emergency space blankets. Why would we need that stuff for a day hike? We did bring a topographical map because it weighed nothing.

George was right, to a point. For the first three miles there was no snow and the trail was easy to follow. Then the trail started to rise, climbing gradually as we headed east. As the trail rose, so did the depth of the snow, and the trail was becoming more difficult to follow. The trail-marking blazes on the trees were sometimes hidden beneath deep snow. But, hey, we had our topo map. When we got to feeling a little uncertain about where we were and where the trail was, we would pull out the map and survey the surrounding peaks, looking for landmarks. By noon the snow was getting really deep, with drifts well over six feet. We came across a long, wide depression that looked like a creek bed. Our topo map showed a creek right about there. We could follow the creek most of the way to the summit.

FLASHBACK: We can hear the water in the creek gurgling beneath the snow. George suggests that we follow the creek, and he starts to walk on the deep snow right up the middle of the creek. That is a bad idea! The snow bridge collapses beneath him. As he falls he screams and spread-eagles his arms wide, arresting his fall. Now he is in the snow up to his chest, dangling ten feet above an icy stream. His eyes are bulging and his mouth is agape. He looks like a man facing imminent death. I grab a spruce branch, lie on my belly and crawl as close as I can without getting out on the bridge myself. No sense both of us going into that hole. I kick my toes into the snow for traction. George grabs the end of the branch and slowly, carefully pulls himself up and across to me. He is shaken. "George, we are not going to walk on top of that freaking creek bed. Let's just stay a few yards on the uphill side of it." We have been spared a disaster and have had a lesson in humility.

We followed a more prudent, if much more difficult, route up the mountain, staying about 20 yards to the north of the creek, on a hillside that sloped sharply uphill, away from the creek. We could still follow the creek, but in a safer position. Every few steps one of us would break through the crust of the snow and end up post-holed on one leg up to his knee or crotch. It was very slow going, slogging along as we climbed up the mountain through deep snow. We had eaten all of our snacks, our feet were soaking wet and we were getting weary. Thoughts of hypothermia entered my head, our remains eaten by bears. Maybe they would find our sneakers in the spring. By three in the afternoon we were no place near the top.

The Sierra Nevada Mountains were formed by the collision of two tectonic plates, with the Pacific Plate on the west pushing up and over the continental plate. The result is that the western slope of the Sierra rises gently from just above sea level to, in many places, well above 10,000 feet. Because the rise is so gentle, it is a much longer slog to the summit. The other side of the Sierra Nevada, the eastern slope, drops off much more steeply. To get the east side George and I would have to cross Kearsarge Pass. We finally made it to the pass at five thirty in the afternoon. That was a half hour past when we were supposed to meet Marty and we still had a distance to go. In the flats just east of the pass we came across a cross-country skier who had just left Onion Valley. He told us that the trailhead was just a mile in front of us, all downhill, and that a very anxious Marty was waiting for us there. We got there at six-thirty, more than an hour late. Marty gave us a tongue lashing, which we deserved for our stupidity and hubris. He was ready to call out a search party if we didn't show up soon.

We went into town, had a spaghetti dinner and a couple of beers, and fell into bed at the motel, totally wiped out. The next day we were up early enough to have a big breakfast and make it to the start of the Wild, Wild West Marathon on time. Still weary from yesterday's snow slog, I ran an unspectacular marathon, finishing not far from last. George? Even after yesterday's misadventure, George finished in second place. Go figure!

A MARATHON EXPERIMENT

The folks at Marathon and Beyond Magazine asked me if I would be interested in trying out a different approach to marathon running. Would I mind, they asked, if I could run the Portland Marathon using a formula that involved intermittent running and walking to a fixed time schedule. One of the premiere marathon gurus had theorized that properly done, this approach would result in a finishing time quite close to running the full distance, and recovery would be much quicker. Being a very cooperative and curious fellow, I told them that I would take the project on.

It was really quite simple: I would run 25 minutes at my normal marathon pace, then walk five minutes at a reasonably fast pace. On race day I followed the instructions to a tee. The results were pretty much as advertised: my time was not much slower and I did recover more quickly. But frankly, I did not enjoy the process very much. It seemed unnatural. I wanted to run when my body told me to run and to walk when I needed to walk. It did not make sense to me to be walking the downhill sections. Still, it was a learning experience. I wrote it up and handed the results in. But I decided not to do that again.

RUNNING MARATHON AS A TOURIST

Where in the world do you want to travel? Odds are that wherever it is, there is a marathon in that area, and they are usually held in the best time of the year. Tens of thousands of runners travel to the big ones like New York, London, Los Angeles and Paris. I am certain that the Chambers of Commerce in those cities are overjoyed with the money they bring in to hotels and restaurants. The entry fee might be a few dollars (over a hundred for the most popular ones), but spending a few nights at a hotel, eating at restaurants will have you dropping at least a thousand dollars in conjunction with your tip-toeing 26 miles. Among the many of us with guilty consciences (for long term emotional neglect of family because of time spent running instead of relating), you might consider bringing your loved one along. It will be a form of payback involving theater tickets and a shopping spree. Multiply that by 10,000 runners and it is easy to see the accountants at the New York Hilton, Macy's, Broadway's theaters and the Stage Deli drooling. I would not be surprised if the New York Marathon brings more than $15,000,000 to the City over that weekend. So what? Spend the money, you earned it. Enjoy yourself; you are doing what you love to do and you can't take it with you.

You don't like big city marathons? There are marathons in every state and many smaller cities in the USA and throughout the world today. Better yet, steer away from the messy urban events altogether. How about the Great Wall of China? The Antarctic? Death Valley? No problem! Chances are that whatever locale you might like to visit, there is a running event waiting for you there, maybe even a marathon.

There are so many marathon options available that you can cherry pick. One of the problems you will have is deciding which ones not to run, there are so many inviting events calling your name.

***

HITTING THE DREADED WALL.

The phrase "hitting the wall" can make the hardiest of runners cringe in fear. In essence, when you 'hit the wall' it means that your fuel tanks have been drained empty, you are out of gas. The readily accessible glycogen that you normally have stored in your bloodstream, muscles and liver is gone, kaput, finito: you have spent it. Your body no longer has enough easily available energy to continue running fast. Now you have to burn fat and muscle, a much slower and more difficult biological task. You find yourself reduced to just putting one foot in front of the other, struggling to do that. It is not an illness, it is not permanent, and it is not especially painful. It is a temporary condition that can be relieved in a short time by taking in something to eat and drink, maybe an energy bar or a Coke, but once you have 'bonked' you will probably not feel chipper very soon.

The wall has a way of showing up someplace around the twentieth mile of a marathon. Modern runners delay or avoid the wall by ingesting energy drinks at critical points in the race, and of course, by proper training. A whole industry has been built on magic formulae for items to ingest before, during and after a marathon or any other strenuous workout. Gatorade was one of the first on the scene, but there are now so many that it has become confusing. Some may even be dangerous. Another element in putting off the wall is to eat lots of carbohydrates during the critical 'tapering' period in the days before a marathon, the commonly used term is 'carbohydrate loading.'

Even more important than caloric intake during a marathon is water. Drinking enough water is critical, both during your training, and immediately before, during and after a marathon. During most marathon races there are frequent aid stations that serve both energy drinks and water. Don't blow by them! The colorful Walter Stack used to put it this way: *"If you ain't peeing, you ain't drinking enough."*

What is my own approach? I like the idea of increasing carbohydrate intake late in my taper week, in the last three days before an endurance event like a marathon, ultra-marathon or triathlon. If the race is on a Sunday, a pasta dinner on Friday is the key meal, no alcohol. *But do not eat like a pig, because it will do you more harm than good.* Make sure to get a lot of sleep. During a long race, take in water at every aid station, even if just a sip. In the later stages of the race something with water, caffeine and sugar comes in very handy. That might be Coke, Pepsi (both watered down) or a cup of sugary tea. And do not forget to refill your tank soon after draining your reserves immediately after the race: It's celebration time! There are magic formulae on what you should have as a post race meal, delineating specific proportions of carbos, fat and protein, along with expensive commercial products to supply your needs and enrich the manufacturers. My advice is to eat what your body tells you it needs.

In the 1960s ultra-running guru Tom Osler preached the importance of the three components that will get you through a long run: water, sugar and caffeine, all of which can be found in a cup of sweet tea or a cola drink. No magic.

(In the next chapters you will read about ultra-marathons and super-marathons. Common wisdom has it that the wall in a 50 mile race arrives at about 35 miles. In a super-marathon the critical time might come be the morning of the fourth day. But remember, we are all different.)

Thousands of runners starting the Havana Marabana Marathon, just before the deluge started.

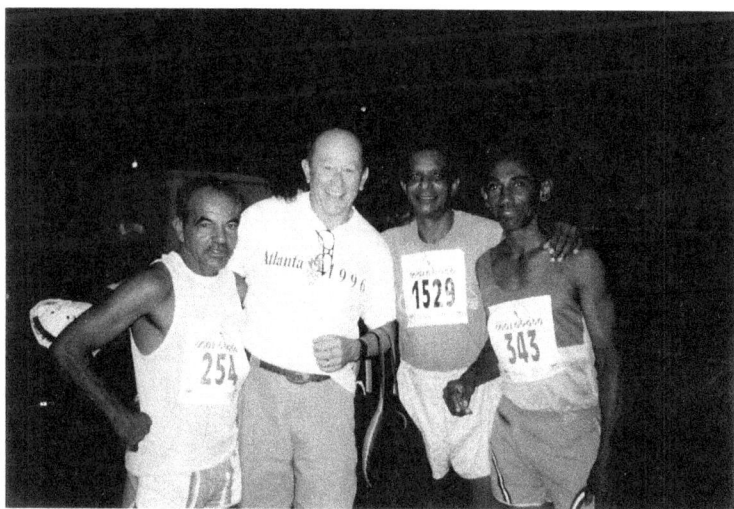

Friendly Cuban runners welcomed us. I am the bald-headed one. We brought several pairs of our old running shoes. The gesture was much appreciated.

These young Cuban ladies ran the marathon barefoot.

The scenery in the Antarctic was magnificent.

I am finishing the 1980 Livermore Marathon, unaware that the runner I had paced died not far from the finish.

On Beyond Marathons: ULTRAMarathons: Part One

"All the performances of human art, at which we look with praise or wonder, are instances of the restless force of perseverance, incessantly continued, in time will surmount the greatest difficulties by the slender force of human beings."
– Samuel Johnson

"We live in a world that is full of beauty, charm and adventure. There is no end to the adventures that we can have if only we seek them with our eyes open."
– Jawaharlal Nehru

During the early days of the labor movement, when workers were fighting for basic working conditions and a decent wage, one of the prominent labor leaders of the day, Samuel Gompers, was asked what labor would want 100 years hence. His answer was that workers would want exactly what they wanted at that time: More.

Some of us belong to that sub-species of the human race that will never be satisfied with our accomplishments. Regardless of what we have done, we will always feel that we must strive for more, ever more. So it is with many long distance runners. We will always feel the compulsion to run a little further than we have already run, beyond our previous best and longest. We want to know, "What is it like beyond that next door, that next mile? And what might happen after that?"

A few years ago I had the pleasure of visiting with the Tarahumara Indians in Copper Canyon, Mexico. They live quietly, a gentle, secluded life in the mountains of central Mexico, where they live off the land. Centuries ago they were driven into the Sierra by invading Spaniards who wanted their gold, their land and their labor. In the protection of the mountains they developed a semi-nomadic lifestyle that brings them to the lush valley lowlands each winter, and to the cooler highlands in summer. They move long distances on foot. The Tarahumara are known worldwide as fine ultra-distance runners. (You can read about them in Born To Run, a fascinating story by Christopher McDougall.) Like 'aloha,' the Tarahumara word "Kiura" has many meanings, all of them friendly. Today, sadly, these innocents are being set upon by narcotics gangs who have seized much of their land for drug farming and forced many of them into servitude.

Chapter 5
ON BEYOND MARATHONS: ULTRAMARATHONS

By 1978 I had run a bunch of marathons and felt that I had that distance well within my control. (Pardon me while I pat myself on the back, but I had become, *ahem, a real marathoner! And we marathoners surely stood head and shoulders above mere mortals.*) I was inflated with my marathon-ismo. I looked forward to the joy and challenge of entering new marathons on unfamiliar courses in distant places. Every marathon race, whether it was a huge and famous one like the Boston or New York or Moscow Marathon with thousands of runners, or a smaller one like the remote Avenue of the Giants, presented another opportunity for me to build up my resume and my ego. I was awed by the fact that it was within my power to transport my body across 26 miles of terrain in almost any part of the world.

Then, at breakfast after one of Joe Henderson's Saturday morning LSD runs (Long, Slow Distance) I overheard Ron Kovacs utter a word that was new to me: ultramarathon. Ron, a strong runner and very knowledgeable about the nooks and crannies of the world of distance running, explained to me that people actually raced at distances longer than the standard 26-mile marathon, and these rare and unusual events were called *ultramarathons*. "How long is an ultramarathon?" I asked. Ron replied that an 'ultra' can be any distance longer than a marathon, from 50 kilometers to … the sky's the limit. Then the sly fox deftly baited the trap. He quietly let on that he was training for the Western States 100 Mile run, coming up the next summer, and he gently reeled me into his web. My illusion that the marathon was the cat's meow, the ultimate accomplishment, was destroyed. I was shocked to learn that people actually ran almost four times that distance. Ron added that ultra-marathons are not really that rare outside the United States. "In fact there is one ultra-marathon race in South Africa, *The Comrades*, that draws over 10,000 entrants every year." I wondered how it was that I had never heard about this.

"Would you like to join me in my training for the Western States, Joe?" said the spider to the fly. "Ron Kovacs, you are nothing but a great big trouble maker! How can I possibly say no?"

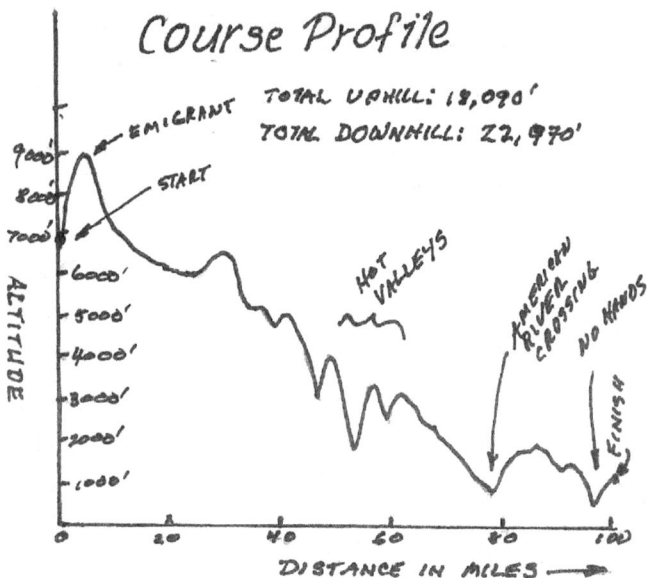

Course Profile

TOTAL UPHILL: 18,090'
TOTAL DOWNHILL: 22,970'

Western States 100 mile run

THE WESTERN STATES 100 MILE RUN

In a marathon you run 26.2 miles, and for most people that means about 30,000 foot-strikes on the ground, step after step, seemingly ad infinitum. Ron and I were joined in our training by John Lehrer, Scott Jackson and John Ullate. Others joined us from time to time. We gradually increased our weekly training mileage, ramping up from about 50 miles a week towards 100 and more. The biggest change was in our weekly longest run, usually on a Saturday. Over several months we increased the distance of the Saturday run to over 20 miles, then 30, then 40 or 50. Because the Western States is 100% on mountain trails, we did most of our training mileage in the mountains of Northern California's Coastal Range. Access to those trails was just minutes from where we lived. A typical run early in our training would take us from Rancho San Antonio Park to the top of Black Mountain, a climb of well over 1,000 feet, some of it on good paths, some of it on narrow, rutted deer trails. We were running just above the San Francisco suburban communities in Silicon Valley, a large population center, but just a few miles to the west we were in truly wild country. There were plenty of deer and rabbits, and where you find deer and rabbits you often find mountain lions and coyotes, which we occasionally spotted as we ran the trails for hours on end. Later in our training we were doing 50 mile trail runs every other weekend, starting in Silicon Valley, crossing the coastal mountains to the Pacific Ocean.

When you are running on trails for several hours, you need water and food. We each carried a couple of quarts of water in belts tied around our waists. Sometimes we would stash gallon milk bottles of water for refills at places where the trail crossed a road. On a rare occasion we would drink from mountain streams, gambling that it would be free of giardia and other unpleasantness. A fanny pack had room for high-energy food like nuts, chocolate, baked potatoes, energy bars, trail mix or a peanut butter sandwich. We were always experimenting with food that would take us through our runs. There was also room for other essentials like toilet tissue, band-aids and a bandana. Lee Jebian was expert at finding fruit trees in season, and there were plenty of them along some of our formerly agricultural routes. We would raid apricot or peach trees that leaned over the rural roads (it is legal), and I learned how to eat prickly pears, a wild edible cactus, without being skewered by their fine spines.

Our 50 mile training runs were sometimes a comedy of errors, and they were always interesting. One time Mark Birdsong and I set out to run to the coast. We had not brought enough food, and by the time we got halfway we were famished. It was a case of "I thought that *you* were bringing the food." Mark suggested that we detour through a picnic ground in a state park, where we came upon a group of very large Samoans having a party. When we, sweaty and dirty, started to approach their party, a pair of 300 pound guys intercepted us. Mark, a quick talking ex-Marine, flashed his broad smile and made quick peace with them, and explained that we were in the middle of a 50 mile run and that we were very hungry. 'Hungry' was something they could relate to, and they invited us to join them. After partaking of their roast pig, pie and a couple of beers, we were on our way again to shouts of 'good luck' from our new patrons. Fifteen miles later, naturally, we were hungry again. On a road near the coast we came across a firehouse with fresh baked pies cooling on the window sill. The smell was irresistible and we were drawn in. Mark told me to run ahead and wait for him. Ten minutes later he caught up with me and we sat behind a gas station eating freshly baked apple pie. "Don't ask." I didn't ask.

On another 50 mile training run, five of us ran from Silicon Valley to the coast. We were scheduled to be met in an ocean-side parking lot by John Warren, who was to bring us food and drive us home. Our group got to the meeting place a little early. John was not there. It was cold and we were tired and hungry. There was a strong, chilly wind coming off the Pacific. I was assigned the job of scouting for food while we waited for John. My first mistake was to approach a group of Girl Scouts, who, after one look at me, a dirty, semi-clad, disreputable looking man, fled away screaming. I then spotted a romantic looking young couple, arms around each other's waist, gazing out at the ocean. I told them that we were hungry and asked if they had any food that they could spare. Not thinking quite straight, I reached inside the front of my shorts for the five-dollar bill that I had hidden there. My gesture was interpreted as something very lewd, but before the guy could throw a punch I pulled out the five dollar bill and quickly explained that I just wanted to buy any food that they might be willing to part with. When they stopped laughing he told me that this was the last day of their California honeymoon, and that they would be flying back to Kokomo, Indiana that evening. He opened the trunk of his car and pulled out a picnic basket that their hotel manager had given them, filled with San Francisco treats: Italian hard salami, a loaf of sourdough bread, a bottle of Napa Valley cabernet sauvignon and some fresh fruit. "You can have this. We can't take it back to Kokomo." I thanked the young lovers and took the basket into the shelter of a drainage ditch, where my starving buddies were huddled. While we were wolfing it down the Girl Scouts shyly came to us, remorseful at their initial lack of generosity, and offered us our dessert: s'mores and Girl Scout cookies. When John Warren arrived he was astonished at the largesse that we had accumulated.

One of the requirements for entry into the Western States race is to run a qualifying 50-miler. In the winter of 1978 there were very few 50 mile runs anywhere, and none were scheduled for Northern California. But a guy named Jack Leydig was putting on an annual event that was called The Christmas Relays, a 50 mile, seven person *relay* that ran south along the ocean on California Highway One, from Half Moon Bay to Santa Cruz. John Lehrer and I asked Leydig if we could enter as solo runners, and he declined. So we each entered the race as a full seven person team. I used the names: Joseph Oakes, Joe Oakes, J. A. Oakes, J. Andrew Oakes, etc. Our entry fees were accepted. That was our very first ultra, and John and

I made a good showing of it, even though we finished far behind the seven person relay teams. We liked the idea so well that we decided to continue the concept in future years on our own. We called it *The Recover From The Holidays Fat Ass Fifty Mile Run*. The rules we established for the Fat Ass 50 are simple: No entry fee; no awards; no big deal; no aid stations along the way; no sponsors; no other rules: You just run your 50 miles and suck it up. Oh, yeah, at the beginning of the run each runner tosses an old tee shirt into a cardboard box. The first finishers got first choice of the shirts in the box. Every year I get calls from people who want to produce a Fat Ass run in their area. My comment is simply, "Go for it." The Fat Ass Fifty concept, our bastard child, has spread to more than 50 locations, including places like Siberia, Holland, England and all over the USA.

Qualifying for the Western States run was the easy part. Training physically and mentally for an effort that would have us running from five in the morning, all day and through the night, up and down mountains, finishing before five the next morning was a terrifying prospect. John Lehrer and I were pretty close in running ability, so we trained together. The Western States was all John and I could talk about. We were obsessed with our impending 100 mile run. John came up with a plan that might help us get our heads screwed on right: We mentally adopted the identities of the two top finishers from the previous year's Western States race, Andy Gonzales and Frank Bozanich. John transformed himself into Andy and I became Frank, and those were the identities into which we transformed ourselves when we trained and strategized. Our play acting took some of the edge off the very hard preparation. The other runners who trained with us thought that we were a bit nuts when we asked them to call us Frank and Andy, but they played along.

Eventually we had to face the music: the Western States was coming up in a couple of weeks. John arranged to rent a house near the ski resort in Alpine Meadows, California, a few miles from the race start at Squaw Valley. That way we could train on the actual mountain trails that make up the course. It was a good idea to go up a week early to acclimatize to the altitude: much of the race is above 7,000 feet, especially the first half. We did daily exploratory runs on different parts of the trail so it would become familiar territory. The last two days before the race we rested and stuffed ourselves with carbohydrates, the best of which was spaghetti with Sylvia's secret sauce. We were Frank Bozanich and Andy Gonzales and we were ready to go.

'Frank and Andy' reported to the check-in the day before the race (signing in under our real names, of course). We took the required physical exam, a very important part of which was the weigh-in. There would be check points during the race where we would have to have our weight again checked by medics. The rules stated that if a runner dropped too much weight at any check point during the run we would have to sit and eat and drink until we gained back enough weight to be allowed to continue running. (In retrospect, sitting and eating and drinking: how bad can that be?)

At five a.m. the next morning the starter's pistol sent about 100 of us running up from the floor of Squaw Valley to the 9,000 foot top of Emigrant Pass, thousands of feet above the valley. It was a brutal start for a hundred mile race. As we ascended in the early morning, the temperature was near freezing. We were prepared for the cold, wearing an old pair of disposable socks for mittens. When we finally got to the top, we continued down the far side heading west. It would be up and down one mountain after another, all that day and through the following night. On the way down from Emigrant Pass a fly on a pine tree could hear, "How ya doin', Andy," followed by "Great Frank, how about you?" We were Frank and Andy and we were on our way.

The total change of elevation could be stated in vertical miles rather than thousands of feet. For me, the most difficult part of the daytime portion of the race was a series of three deep valleys at lower altitudes after we passed the 50 mile point. On the valley floors the temperature was almost 100 F. Frank and Andy slogged and sweated up and down them, drinking a lot of water, sometimes climbing at almost a crawl. We came out of the forest at a check point in a small village, Foresthill, about 65 miles into the race. At that point we had gone two thirds of the way with still about 35 miles, well over a marathon, to go. It was getting late in the day. A significant percentage of the runners often have an attack of sanity at Foresthill and call it quits. Not Andy and Frank. We had run together this far and our support crews were there to meet and pace us the rest of the way during the night. My pre-ordered banana milk shake and pineapple pizza were waiting for me, and after the compulsory weigh-in and a ten minute break, we were off again, headed into the black of night in the forest. Somehow at that point Andy and Frank lost contact with each other in the dark. We would not see each other again until the end of the race.

That last third of the race is mostly at around 3,000 feet elevation, but it is in dense forest and it is still all uphill and downhill, with plenty of 500 foot rises and falls. Under the tree cover, the night was pitch black, and the trail was very narrow and easy to lose, with lots of roots and rocks to trip you. There was a full moon, but not much of its light made it through the trees. We used flashlights and carried extra batteries, but running with a flashlight, the beam bouncing up and down on a narrow trail is dicey. Uneven ground jumps up to trip you and low branches spring down to slap your face. The pace slows considerably. Once in a while you might spot the bouncing flashlight of another runner ahead in the distance, or behind you if you look back.

Where the trail crosses the American River, a sturdy, two inch thick rope is stretched between jeeps on either side on either side of the river so runners do not get swept away in the swift, icy current. You grab the rope with both hands, on the upstream side of the river and wade as you pull your way across water that gets to about four feet deep in places. The cold water was refreshing, as was the dry pair of shoes and socks that I had stowed on the other side. From there it was up another steep rise, past the Highway 49 aid station, and down to the American River again, this time crossing the river on 'No-Hands Bridge,' with no handrails in the middle of the inky night, high above the canyon.

Flashback: I have been running for almost 20 hours. Intellectually I know that the last grizzly bear was killed in California over 100 years ago, but I am certain that I see one hiding in the trees, waiting to jump me and eat me. Reliable, steady Scotty Jackson, who is pacing me, tries to calm me by assuring me that there is no bear, but I look up and see another goddamned grizzly bear peering hungrily and menacingly down the slope above me. Scotty tells me that I am hallucinating, and not to worry about it: "It is not unusual to hallucinate under these conditions." "Then what is that goddamned thing with big red eyes on the trail ahead of us?" Scotty jollies me on. What would I do without him? I focus on trying to stay vertical and putting one foot in front of the other. To hell with the frigging bears!

Narrow No-Hands-Bridge is not a good place to be in the dark when you are overly fatigued and wobbly. There are no guard rails, and it is a long fall down into the boulder-strewn American River below. Scotty took me by the hand like a Boy Scout taking a granny across the street in heavy traffic. When I looked at my watch after crossing No-Hands-Bridge I was in tears. It was after three in the morning. I had planned my detailed schedule to finish before five AM, just under 24 hours, so I could earn the rare, cherished silver belt buckle. My feeble mental calculations told me that I could no longer make it to the finish line at Auburn High School by five. I pushed on as hard as I could, but there was not much left in the tank and still miles to go. I was blubbering. *"What the hell are you going on about, Joe?"* Scotty could not understand that I was trying to tell him that I had failed. Up the American Canyon trail we ran, and into the outskirts of the town of Auburn. *"You are doing fine, Joe. Just a quarter mile and you will be on the track and it will be all over."* We ran through the darkened streets of the city of Auburn to the high school grounds, through a gate and onto the quarter mile track. When I finally rounded the last curve of the track to the finish line at Auburn High School, I looked up at the overhead digital clock and was shocked to see that I had made it in just over 23 hours. I had finished with almost an hour to spare: my confused, sleep-deprived brain had taken an hour more to get there than my legs did. And the grizzly bears didn't get me.

Not far behind me John Lehrer came toddling onto the track, looking like the cat that had eaten the canary, the goldfish and all of Garfield's lasagna. There were hugs all around, even if it was four in the morning. A reunited Andy and Frank took their famished bodies to Denny's restaurant nearby and ordered food, more food, and then even more. A shower, a nap, and a few minutes in the hot tub fixed us up for the awards ceremony and a pair of silver belt buckles. John pointed out that throughout the history of the race only 15 of those rare silver belt buckles had ever been earned prior to our race. I took off my sweaty bandana and ostentatiously buffed my prize.

FLASHBACK: I am hungry, very, very, hungry. I am empty, completely drained of energy after running 100 miles. My tank and my reserve tank are empty. I'm not just hungry: I would fight a cougar for food. Every part of me is starving. My fingernails, my skin, my teeth are all screaming for food, lots of food, right now! I will eat anything put in front of me then want more. It will be too long before my digestive system is able to process enough food to satisfy me, so keep it coming. The attentive waitress at Denny's recognizes the syndrome: the restaurant is not far from the finish of the Western States Trail and she has fed food-needy ultra-runners before. The food starts coming fast and it goes down my gullet just as fast. Pancakes! Bacon and eggs! Orange juice! More, more, more!

In a marathon a runner may burn about 3,000 calories. That is not much more than a normal day's intake of food. Much of what your body burns comes from the glycogen that you have stored in your liver, blood and muscles, and it can be supplemented by taking in a limited amount of energy foods like Gatorade. After a marathon you can refill your tanks with one big meal. In a 100 mile run, especially one that is all mountains, you will probably burn more like four of five days of normal food intake. Your body simply cannot store that amount of glycogen for you. You know that you are going to go deep into energy debt. After you have depleted your stored glycogen, your body will next start to burn available body fat, the next easiest fuel it can find. That will carry you a few more miles. But body fat burns more slowly than glycogen so you will be forced to slow down. If you go much further into energy debt your furnace will start burning muscle cells, including your heart. Did I say something about being hungry?

And when your race is finished, you have an inordinate desire to stoke up, to refuel. The unfortunate thing is that no matter how much you eat, your digestive apparatus can only convert food at a limited rate: your internal machinery can only digest food so fast. Filling the void takes time. Eat what you can and enjoy it, but know that you will still feel hungry no matter how much you eat.

I competed in the Western States Trail Run three times. It is a beautiful, mystical course, in a huge and powerful place. If you have the opportunity to run just a few miles of the Western States Trail you will understand the strong feelings of connection that it brings back to me, so many years later. John Muir had a love affair with all the earth, but he particularly loved the Sierra Nevada Mountains. "*The grand show is eternal. It is always sunrise somewhere. The dew is never dried at once. A shower is falling. Vapor is ever rising. Eternal sunrise, eternal sunset. Eternal dawn and glowing, on sea and continents and islands, each in its turn as the earth rolls. And for all of this I am grateful to be alive.*"

"*Sweet is pleasure after pain*" said John Dryden. But Dryden never ran an ultra-marathon. Immediately on finishing an ultra the almost universal comment is "I will never do that again." It is only after the cessation of pain, and that might take days or even weeks, that the memory of agony slowly seeps away. Then you will be ready to look back on the pleasurable aspects of your achievement. That is when you start toying with the idea of your next session of self-abuse.

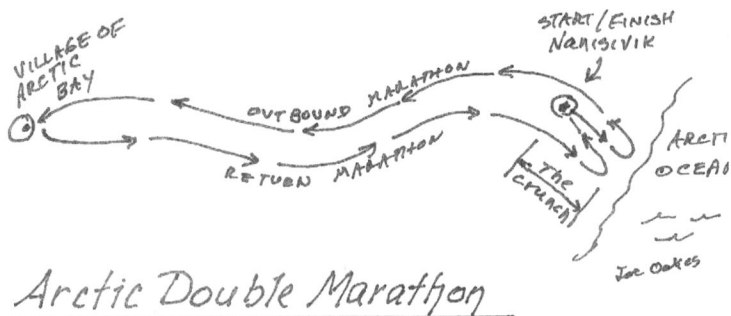

Arctic Double Marathon

AN ARCTIC ULTRA: NANISIVIK

The Western States 100 mile run billed itself as *The Ultimate Running Challenge*. I told myself that maybe the word 'ultimate' was a bit of an exaggeration. All you had to do was add another mile or so, or another 1,000' of elevation change, or maybe put it into an even more remote locale and it would get a wee bit closer to being the 'ultimate running challenge.' I was beginning to get the feeling that I had done all the running that I wanted to do. In order to become motivated to put any real effort into my training I would have to find a new challenge. Then, in the schedule section of *Ultrarunning Magazine* I came across a listing for a double marathon, an 84 kilometer race that would be held 1,000 kilometers north of the Arctic Circle, on the north end of Baffin Island. The race was scheduled to be held on Canada Day, July 1. That looked like an interesting challenge to get me motivated again. And what a place for a *double marathon*! Canada is the second largest nation in the world after Russia. (The USA is fourth, behind China.) The distance from Toronto to the top of Baffin Island is comparable to the distance across the USA. I knew very little about the Arctic, but I sure wanted to try this adventure. I was entertaining visions of polar bears, Eskimos, sub-zero temperatures and deep, deep snow.

I contacted the Toronto race director, 'Arctic Joe' Womersley, to see if he still had room for me. He told me that there were still a few places, and that not many Americans would be there. I booked a flight to Toronto where I joined a planeload of runners on a charter flight to Baffin Island. On board was a great group of fun-loving Canadians, and they welcomed this Yank into their midst. Up and down the aisle strode our sixtyish, light-hearted race director, making friends with every runner on board, seeing to their comfort and allaying their fears. 'Arctic Joe' also did a commendable job of passing out drinks on the very long flight, paying particular attention to the ladies on board. There was a lot about twinkly-eyed, impish Womersley that you had to love.

Our destination was an Inuit village called *Nanisivik*, where Strathcona Minerals operated a large underground lead-silver-zinc mine, served by ocean-going bulk cargo ships. The ships could only land there in a narrow window of a few days in late August when the sea ice was finally out. In the Inuit language Nanisivik means 'the place where you find things,' and Strathcona had surely found a bonanza. To serve the mine they had built infrastructure, including a school, a swimming pool, a gravel airstrip, and a road to the nearest town, Arctic Bay, about 20 miles west across Baffin Island. Baffin Island is roughly the size and shape of California, almost 1000 miles long north and south. After refueling at Frobisher Bay in the south of Baffin Island, the big plane circled the Nanisivik's airfield three times before the pilot brought it in on a purely visual approach: the tiny airfield was not equipped for instrument landings.

Starkly beautiful is the best way to describe northern Baffin Island. We were hundreds of miles north of the tree line, well above the Arctic Circle, with only an occasional dwarf willow in evidence. From Frobisher Bay in the south to Nanisivik in the north, Baffin Island is covered with rugged mountains. There are accumulations of centuries-old snow in places where the howling winter wind can't sweep it away. This is a sparsely populated arctic desert with little snowfall, but what snow does fall stays for a long time. The island is incapable of offering much support to plant or animal life. But life tenaciously hangs on, with arctic hares, wolves, foxes, caribou, musk oxen and polar bears. From the sea the Inuit harvest fish, seals, whales and narwhals. Migratory waterfowl nest on Baffin Island every summer, returning south when the northern days start to shorten.

Most of the mine's employees were from the populated areas in the south in Canada, many of them from Newfoundland, but there was no shortage of Inuit. (The term 'Eskimo' was considered politically incorrect in Canada, but not among the Eskimos in Alaska.) Our lodgings were in workers barracks or with the families of miners and Inuit. Many of the Newfoundland miners had returned home for their summer holiday.

We arrived late in the evening, but it was broad daylight: the July sun would be with us 24 hours a day. After being assigned to beds and having a few welcome drinks, I hit the sack under the bright sky at about eleven in the evening. (Here is a tip about sleeping when the sun is bright: Tie a bandana around your head to shield your eyes. It works.) But the sunlight was not what prevented me from getting some shuteye: Throughout the night the Inuit kids were making the usual noises that kids make when playing. In the high Arctic it makes no difference whether it is noon or three in the morning. When you live in a place where there is no such thing as a 24 hour day, normal diurnal life has no meaning: It's dark half the year and bright the other half. Kids and adults just go about their business regardless of what a clock might say. So, if there is no day or night, what about mealtimes? There are no mealtimes as we know them. One Inuit explained to me that there was always a big chunk of raw seal or walrus meat on his table. When you want something to eat you just slice off a slab and eat it raw. (Thus the origin of the Athabaskan Indian word, 'Eskimo', which in their language means 'eater of raw flesh.')

The town is on a high bluff above an arm of the Arctic Ocean. Far, far below the village is a huge storage building where the ore waits for the transport ships to take it away in August. The 200 meter long building was so far down the hill that it looked small. A runner who had been here before said, "Take a look down there. *That* is The Crunch." I did not understand what he was talking about. I would find out soon enough.

Arctic Joe called a meeting to tell us about the course. "It is 20 miles from here to Arctic Bay. You will be running there and back." Someone asked how 40 miles added up to a double marathon. Joe grinned and told us, "You are right, so both before and after your round trip we have a really nice diversion for you. It is called The Crunch, a six mile round trip down the mountain from here to the shoreline and back up. You will do The Crunch before starting from Nanisivik to Arctic Bay, and you will do all six miles of The Crunch again when you get back to Nanisivik." 52 miles of running in the Arctic, with the brutal Crunch for openers and closers!

We were given the option of running a single marathon or the double. Most of us were experienced marathon runners, with a handful of ultra-runners among us. For several, this talk about The Crunch helped them to make a big decision: The 42 kilometer (26 mile) single marathon would be enough. Our group split in two, about one third opted for the longer run and the rest for the marathon.

Then Joe made his final announcement. "We ultra-marathon runners will start running down and up the Crunch from here at 0500 tomorrow morning. When we get to Arctic Bay we will turn around and do it all over again in the opposite direction. I will be running in the first group." He paused, then he addressed the marathon runners. "You other wimpy bastards will leave from here by bus to Arctic Bay at 0700. You will pass us en route. Your race starts in Arctic Bay at 0800. You will run back here to Nanisivik and finish your marathon with a Crunch."

We heroic 'ultra' guys came together for an early breakfast and were ready for the 0500 start. It was July 1, Canada Day, and the race was to be started by a uniformed Royal Canadian Mounted Police officer, the only policeman in that immense part of the northern world. The crisp Arctic air was still and clear and the temperature was just below freezing. A crowd of about 50 sleepy family members, Inuit and miners gathered to cheer us on our long slog. I suspect that the spectators went back to bed after we left the camp. The Mountie raised his pistol, and slowly counted 3-2-1 BOOM! We were on our way down the Crunch.

I would like to describe the frenzied start, the heightened adrenalin, the initial sprint to be first. Instead I will tell the truth. We all knew that we would be out there running for a very long time, and that there would be lots of time to push ourselves hard later. Right now most of us were satisfied that we were moving along at better than a snail's pace, that the weather was mild, and that we were in good company.

In very long races it is really nice to have the company of a compatible runner. Arctic Joe and I ran together for the first part of the race. Going down and then up six miles of The Crunch was a bitch of a way to start a long day, but that was the only thing on the menu, and it was the same for everyone, so why complain? 1,000 knee-killing feet of dropping down The Crunch was followed by 1000 feet of panting lungs humping back up it, and we were now back where we started, ready for the real race across the island. None of the spectators had waited for us to make our round trip Crunch. At one point we were pretty far down the road en route to the turnaround at Arctic Bay when Joe Womersley heard the bus carrying the 'wimpy marathoners' across to their start at Arctic Bay.

FLASHBACK: Arctic Joe takes my arm and says, "Joe, I have to tell you about a tradition we have here. When the marathoner's bus reaches us we block the road. When we have their attention, drop our drawers and we moon them. Then we let them pass."

As the bus rolled up we faced away from them and formed a blockade across the narrow gravel road. On Joe's signal we gave the required salute to the 'wimps' on the busses. Astronomical observatories all over the world noted that on the morning of Canada Day, on the north end of Baffin Island, several pink moons shone simultaneously and were witnessed by a busload of surprised marathon runners.

Running 52 miles is never easy, and we were in an alien environment devoid of trees, cold (but not terribly so), and terrified by the knowledge that when we got back to Nanisivik we still had to run down and up the God-awful Crunch. But you know what?

We did it, each and every starter made it, Crunches and all. And I will tell you why: It was because we were having a good time in the company of some really good people, not just the runners, but the people who has set out gallon jugs of water every mile, and the vacationing miners whose beer supply we (mea culpa) so blithely devoured.

FLASHBACK: "Who the heck is that guy?" I ask Arctic Joe as the bare-chested stranger goes blasting by on his return trip from Arctic Bay. He looks like he doesn't weigh more than 135 pounds. "I'll tell you but you have to promise to keep your big yap shut. His name is Bruce Fordyce and he is from South Africa." I am aware that South African athletes are barred from competing outside of their home country because of their government's policy of 'apartheid.' Joe has secretly arranged for Fordyce to compete in Canada under an alias. Joe informs me that Bruce Fordyce has won the prestigious Comrades race in South Africa several times, and that he is one of the top ultra-runners in the world. Bruce finished the Nanisivik race a full hour ahead of the second place finisher. It is a shame that he has to fake his identity in order to compete.

I wish I could remember all of the runners who made that trip with me. Names and faces come to mind: Margaret Mason; Sy Mah; Bill and Bea Beddor; Kent and B.J. Prizer (who would later put on the Pennsylvania versions of the Fat Ass Fifty); Irishman Vivian Doyle-Kelly; Shane Collins (who later redirected his energies to become a very fine long distance swimmer); Graham Farquarson; Alan and Mary Firth; Rev. Laurie Dexter; Wally Herman and the incomparable Jo Welles with her cheerful husband, "Thoe" Velo Petrauskas. Good people all, people with whom I will always be ready to break bread and trade tall tales. I went back to Nanisivik five times to run and celebrate more Canada Days, and I grunted along more than my belly-full of the 20 mile gravel road going to and from Arctic Bay, and much more than my share of Crunches. Joe Womersley is no longer with us, gone to pester God up in Heaven. Strathcona Minerals sold the mine to a foreign concern that has no tolerance for a bunch of itinerant ultra-marathon runners. Without Joe and Strathcona, the run is no more. Only the wonderful memories remain.

A HOT AND HUMID ULTRAMARATHON

Having enjoyed the hospitality of the folks on Baffin Island in the summer, Alan Firth and I decided to put together an ultramarathon that could be run in the coldest part of the winter, a time when there are not a lot of races to choose from. We got help from Jesse Dale Riley, who lived in Key West, Florida. December was the best time for it because there were virtually no ultra events at that time (unless you counted the rogue Fat Ass Fifty milers.) For convenience, it would have to be at a location reasonably close to a major airport someplace in the east. Florida seemed the obvious choice, and the further south the better. There is a certain cache about Key West, the furthest south that you can go on US Highway 1, so we decided that we would start our run 100 miles north of Key West and run all the way south to finish at milepost zero in Key West. The people in Key West call their home "The Conch Republic." They do not consider themselves a part of the USA or any other country.

If you have ever driven to Key West you are aware that the Florida Keys is a long chain of small islands connected by US 1, a single highway that crosses a lot of bridges. Except for the bridges, it is as flat as a pancake. And it is always hot and humid. The best time of year is December, but even then it can be too hot to run an ultramarathon. To avoid the heat we decided to start the run in the evening at the 100 mile marker in Key Largo so the runners could enjoy the cool night. We called our race the Key to Shining Key 100 Mile Run. The state police gave us permission to start our run on a Saturday evening in early December. Norrie Williamson came from South Africa to survey the course and certify that it was exactly 100 miles long. Norrie is one of the best course measurers in the world. Using a calibrated bicycle he cycled the entire route twice and marked off a course that he certified as exactly 100 miles.

We started the run at five PM on Saturday evening, a time when most people are getting ready for their evening meal. For much of the route there are paths and sidewalks along the side of US 1, but there are some places, such as bridge crossings where pedestrians are exposed to traffic on a narrow shoulder. Some of the runners planned to complete only the first 50 miles, but most had signed on for the 100 mile run all the way to Key West. The first ten miles or so went without incident. It was a balmy evening, a fine night for a casual stroll of 100 miles. The runners paired off with companions who could run at their pace. The slow pace of an ultra-marathon permits relaxed conversation.

Our group ran from key after key, enjoying the quiet warmth of the tropical night until about two AM. That is when the local rednecks started leaving the bars. One of them got the bright idea that it might be fun to throw their empty beer cans at the runners from their cars. That went on until the cops finally broke up their stupid game. On and on they ran down Highway 1, over bridges, across keys and more bridges and more keys. Some time before dawn the first 50 milers arrived at their finish area at Marathon Key. Soon the leading 100 milers were joining them, a good place to take a break before continuing the next 50 miles to Key West. A few of the 100 milers decided wisely that the break at Marathon Key felt so good that they would settle for a 50 miler instead of 100. It was not a bad idea, because it was already getting hot and the day promised to be a scorcher.

The temperature steadily climbed to the low 90s, and the running was becoming very hard. It was late afternoon when the first

100 mile runner, a Floridian, reached Key West. One by one they dragged their weary bodies to the conclusion. There was a minor panic when one of the runners couldn't be located. Some clever detective work eventually found Washingtonian Gary Wright sleeping behind a billboard at the last aid station a few miles out of town. Gary just got up and jogged on in, bravely if sleepily.

We all sat down and gorged ourselves to a Sunday brunch at an all-you-can-eat restaurant. The awards ceremony was held after brunch at a hotel swimming pool. A few of the runners slept right through the awards, completely understandable and forgivable. Every finisher was given a personally decorated conch shell as a souvenir of their hot and humid 100 mile trip to Key West, The Conch Republic. I was never tempted to put on that race again.

THE COW MOUNTAIN FIFTY

There are some races that you just love to remember. The Cow Mountain 50 Miler fits into that category. It was a very hilly, out-and-back trail race held in the remote mountains east of Ukiah, CA.

This race was a man-against-horse race. The human runners were given a half hour start ahead of the mounted horses. The equines started at dawn: we were a half hour down the trail by that time. We also had the advantage of not having to stop for mandatory veterinarian checks. Mark Birdsong, Marti Maricle and I ran the first half together. Marti's plan was to run only the first half, 25 miles.

Mark and I ran reasonably well until, at about mile 40, we took a wrong turn. After a half mile, we knew that we done wrong. When we looked back we could see other runners going up the mountain trail behind us where we had mistakenly gone downhill. Bad mistake! You had better believe that grown men do cry.

You know what? We got our shit together and finished the Cow Mountain 51 (if you count our detour) Mile race. We even got trophies for beating more than half of the horses to the finish line. The best part of it was that trophy, a twelve inch ceramic horse penis that, when inverted, can be used as a beer mug. In the Hash they say that all beer comes from the same horse. Sylvia will not allow me to put my valued trophy on display in our home, despite my hard work in earning it.

By the way, Marti Maricle decided at the turnaround that she would run the entire 50 miles. Marty finished as first place woman in her very first ultra-marathon, and she beat the horses and most of the men.

My Inuit friend, young Philip Quavavaq, at Nanisivik, Baffin Island.

The finish line of the first Fat Ass Fifty at the Upper Crust Pizza in Santa Cruz, 1978.

Training for the Western States 100, carrying a pack. We knew nothing about running ultras. Few people did.

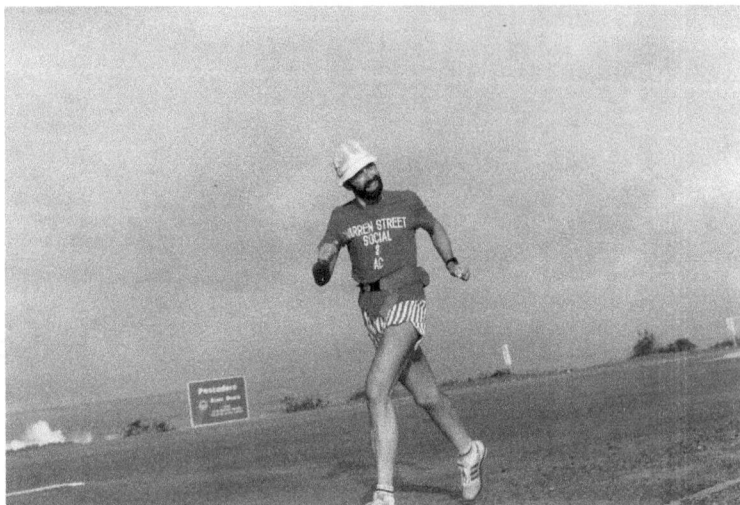

My training partner, the incomparable John Lehrer. We were Andy and Frank.

The original course of the Fat Ass Fifty ran due south along Highway One along the California coast, an inspiring place to run.

Nanisivik: Running with Bill Beddor. I used running socks for mittens in the high arctic.

Nanisivik: A special trophy for five times up-and-down The Crunch. The tee shirt is from the South Bay Hash House Harriers.

Nanisivik: At the Terry Fox cairn.

Arctic Joe Womersley (left) and I in the Yukon.

ULTRAMarathons: Part Two

"They shall mount up with wings as eagles; they shall run and not be weary, and they shall walk and not faint."
– Isaiah, 40:31

"Heroism, the Caucasian mountaineers say, is endurance for one more second."
– George Kennan

To persevere for one more second, one more minute, one more hour: it all comes to just this: the ability to make yourself keep moving right now, despite the pain, the fatigue, and despite the logic of just seeking the comfort of quitting. Call it heroism, courage, endurance, spirit, guts, it's all the same: take one more step, then another, then one more again. No one but you can call that up from the depths of your body and soul.

FLASHBACK: Zion National Park, Utah. I am running on a riverside trail in an overwhelmingly beautiful place. I am alone and that is how I like it in this place. On every side of me cliffs soar straight up thousands of feet to meet a cloudless sky. The colors of the mountains are breathtaking, layered and painted in place over millions of years, compressed into striations, then carefully carved away by wind and water. The dominant color is rust red in 100 shades and blended together with other earth hues.

Sylvia put it this way: "It's like being in the bottom of Grand Canyon looking up into a cathedral that God built and decorated over eternity."

To my left is the Virgin River, a small, fast running river that has been steadily eating away at the foundations of these mountains, one gritty grain at a time. When the snow melts in the spring, the Virgin River grows to a raging torrent, dragging of tons of large boulders and sediment with it every second. The river carries all that sediment across Nevada, through Las Vegas and into the Colorado River near Boulder Dam. Every few years, when the snowmelt is particularly heavy, the Virgin swells high above its banks and tears away the Fremont cottonwood trees growing alongside, taking out roads and any manmade structures built close to it. But right now the Virgin River is tranquil, running downhill, skipping over boulders, forming little pools in backwaters, and making a peaceful gurgling sound.

This is harsh desert country. Life here is difficult and tenuous. But life finds ways to survive. A chattering stellar jay chides me because I am trespassing in his territory. "Don't run here. Go away. This is my forest." I slow my pace as soon as I spot a doe and her fawn nibbling the tender riverside grass not five yards from the trail. A brazen ground squirrel stands on his hind legs to request a handout. He has been spoiled by tourists. Yesterday I looked up and saw something that had been missing from this sky for decades, a California condor: Its wingspan was nine feet or more. If we look around we will find reason to hope.

That is the thing about a place like this: the enormity of the mountains seems to overpower everything, but the small, living things will not be intimidated.

CHAPTER SIX
ULTRAMARATHONS PART TWO

A VERY HOT AND DRY ULTRA: DEATH VALLEY

At 282 feet below sea level, the lowest point in the Western Hemisphere is at Badwater in Death Valley, California; one of the hottest and driest places on earth. On a summer day the temperature normally exceeds 100 F and is frequently measured above 120 F. If you travel west from Death Valley National Park you will cross the Panamint Mountains and enter Lone Pine in the Owens Valley. From Lone Pine there is a road that snakes up to Whitney Portal, at about 8,000 feet. From Whitney Portal there is a foot trail that will take you up to the highest point in the USA outside of Alaska, the top of Mount Whitney, 14,505 feet above sea level. Most of the year there is snow atop Mount Whitney, even in the early summer. I do not know whom to blame, but somebody got the idea, many years ago, to run from Badwater, at the bottom of Death Valley, all the way to the top of Mount Whitney, some 139 miles and more than 14,000 feet higher. To count as a real challenge it had to be done in either July or August, so the temperature would be in the blood-boiling range. Here is one more thing to think about: Once you reach the top of Mount Whitney, maybe at two AM, where the hell are you? You are in a remote place, on the top of a very big mountain, and to get out of there you have to go down more than 6,000 vertical feet of mountain trails to get back to Whitney Portal, the closest road access. That brings your total mileage to about 144 (but the final descent doesn't really count.)

That's a very long way to run across the desert in Death Valley, and a very long way to climb up Mount Whitney. En route you will also have to cross the Panamint Mountains. The temperature will be over 100 F during the day and above 90 F at night. Keep in mind that the sun-baked ground will be egg-frying hot in the Valley and it will be below freezing at the top of Whitney. The good folks at the US Forest Service issue permits to climb Whitney on a first-come-first-served basis. They strongly urge that you start your climb at Whitney Portal, at 8,000 feet, and take two or three days to get from there to the top. They do not know how to deal with the insanity of ultra-runners who want to do the whole darned thing, up and back, in a single day.

This huge challenge can be approached in two ways. You can just do it on your own, without bothering to get a permit (and get a citation for breaking the law if you get caught) or you can enter an organized race. Here is the problem with doing it as part of the formal race: Because of overly conservative Park Service decisions, the race is no longer permitted to run beyond Whitney Portal, so the

Badwater race ends at Whitney Portal. I am not denigrating the race to Whitney Portal: it is one hell of a challenge. But Whitney Portal remains a full 6,000 feet below the original destination, the summit of Mount Whitney.

I have challenged Whitney both ways. I failed in my attempt to compete in the race from Badwater to Whitney Portal. At the start Keith Pippin told us that the air temperature at Badwater was 131 F five feet above the ground, but it did not feel quite that hot. I was dressed in a white Sahara robe with a white hat and neck covering to keep the sun at bay, looking like a comic version of Ahab the A-rab. The gun went off and we started running tentatively, knowing that we had a long, hot day ahead of us. It was not very long before the lead pack was a speck in the distance, far ahead in the clear desert air. I ran at my own pace and was doing reasonably well for the first 80 miles. I had a superb support crew that consisted of my son Chris, experienced ultra-runner John Warren and rugged army paratrooper Colonel Len Wallach. They kept me cool with a steady supply of ice water, both for my innards, and to pour over my head to drip down my long, white Arab costume, cooling me as it evaporated. The temperature of the black road surface reached 150 F that morning, and I, like everyone else, tried to run along the highway's white stripe, which was a little cooler than the blacktop.

FLASHBACK: I feel like I am on a barbecue grill; it is that hot. We have reached the 90 mile marker, and there is an enormous amount of pain in my feet. They feel like they are being flayed. Len Wallach helps me to take off my shoes. Both socks are soaked with blood. John turns away. Chris goes to the van for ice. Len looks at me and says that the callouses on the balls of both feet have become detached and are peeling/ sliding around, well beyond blistering. I load up on ibuprofen and try to keep my skin in place by binding my feet with duct tape: that sometimes works. I thank them and hobble down the road, but the constant pain

101

is making it increasingly difficult to keep pounding and torturing myself with every step on the hot blacktop. The next time I reach the van I black out and collapse. Chris catches me before I hit the broiling asphalt. It is beyond my ability to stay in the race. I never made it to Lone Pine. I had crossed the Valley of Death, but cannot possibly go on to climb the Big Mountain in the Sky.

I can feel sorry for myself for the pain, but my loyal crew suffered almost as much as I did. They sat for long hours in a sweltering van. Air conditioning does not work very efficiently in Death Valley, and an idling car will overheat very quickly with the AC running. They gave a lot for me, trying to keep me going, even as they watched me deteriorate. There are no expressions of appreciation that will suffice.

Did I fail? Yes and no. I can't be unhappy with what I did: I gave it my best. But I did not reach the finish. As the saying goes, you can't win 'em all.

That was that, finished, kaput. But I will always carry one very special and vivid pictorial memory from that race, one that will always remind me of just where I am. I can see myself running along the road in Death Valley, heading straight north on a very dark night. Directly in front of me, through the extremely clear air of the desert, I can focus my attention on Polaris, the North Star, low in the sky, immobile, about 25 degrees above the horizon. As I ran north hour after hour, it became clear that all of the other stars were circling around Polaris, the only star in the heavens that held its ground, never budging up or down, never making circles like the other stars. I watched the Big Dipper making its circle with the other stars, rising and falling above and below the horizon while Polaris just stayed firmly in place. That star, situated in a direct line with the axis of the Earth, points its bright light at where my planet, my solar system and I are situated in this unbelievably enormous and constantly moving universe. That night I counted 17 meteors as they burned themselves out, briefly and brightly dying as they tried to enter Earth's atmosphere.

Notwithstanding my non-finish in the Badwater race, I made it to the top of Mount Whitney three times: With Gary Emich and a group of Post Office employees; With my son, Chris; and with John Warren. I will not try again, ever.

People ask me how one prepares for the unique Badwater Ultramarathon. The answer is that you have to develop a training program that addresses your own strengths and weaknesses and the specific challenges of the race. It must include the following essential elements:

1. A huge amount of running mileage. Most marathon runners put in 50-75 miles a week. That is not nearly enough for Badwater. Consider doubling that number as you approach race day.

2. Hill training is crucial, and the hills have to be very long, and should probably amount to 30-50% of your training mileage.

3. Heat training. How did I prepare for the heat? I did 1,000 sit-ups at a time in the sauna at a local health club. If you live where it is hot, get in your heat training on the road.

4. Cross training. Why? To fend off boredom, and to keep the rest of your body looking pretty. Try to work in some cycling, swimming and trips to the gym.

5. On-the-course training. Take the time to go to Death Valley and, if nothing else, drive the course from Badwater up to Whitney Portal. There is nothing like it anywhere else in the world. Like breaking in a new pair of shoes, make sure that you have mentally "worn" the course before race day.

6. You might consider learning to take short naps in the middle of long runs. Some very good runners do it.

7. Make sure that you have a strong, understanding and dedicated

crew. There may be times in your delirium and wretchedness when you will cuss them out; they will have to give you tough love; and they will be out in that damnable hot sun just as long as you will.

Let me tell you about Marat Zhilanbaev. In his homeland, Kazakhstan, Marat is known as The Camel. He is a national hero. Every morning he runs 13 miles through the desert from his home in Ekibastuz, carrying neither water nor food, to the local airport. At the airport he drinks a couple of liters of water, has a snack, then runs back home, a full marathon every single day, almost 200 miles a week. His claim to fame is that he has run across vast deserts, including the Gobi, the Atacama and the Sahara. His life goal is to cross every major desert in the world. One of the deserts that he wanted to cross was what he called 'Great American Desert', and by that he meant from Four Corners (where AZ, CO, NM and UT meet) all the way to and across Death Valley. He asked me to help him set it up and to run with him.

Marat brought a support crew from the USSR and rented a motor home for the trip. Starting at Four Corners, he ran at least a desert marathon every day, at times bush-whacking across Indian land. My schedule did not permit me to start the journey in Four Corners with his group, but I joined them after they had crossed Arizona and entered Nevada. Once he reached Nevada, Marat became bedazzled by the phenomenon that is Las Vegas. When he learned that prostitution was not illegal in Nevada, it became a big distraction, which we will not go into here. After we got him to re-focus his attention, he went on to run across Nevada and into Death Valley. Midway across the Valley we met up with the guru of running in Death Valley, the *unofficial* Mayor of Death Valley, Doctor Ben Jones. In reality Ben has long served as the *official* coroner in Death Valley. He also has successfully run the entire distance from bottom to top several times. On one occasion Ben rented a hearse and put in an ice-filled coffin to cool himself off during the hottest part of the day.

Marat made it all the way across Death Valley, completing his quest to run the Great American Desert. Then he ran up Mount Whitney, finishing a few miles beyond Whitney Portal. But the spring snow was deep, and though he slogged through it for another mile or so, there was no way that he could get to the top. But he had, in fact, run a marathon a day, all the way across the Great American Desert, from Four Corners through Death Valley. No one else has done that.

The next year Marat entered the Badwater race, finishing second overall. (By the way, the movie "Barat", which is supposed to be about Kazakstan, was actually filmed in an impoverished village in Romania, and had nothing to do with Kazakstan. So it goes, moviegoers.)

Just to prove that there are people who are tougher than tougher than tough, there are a very few, including Rich Benyo, former editor or Runners World, who have run from Badwater to the very top of Mount Whitney and then all the way back down to Badwater, over 300 miles. One unbelievable athlete, Marshall Ullrich, ran up, then down, then up and down again, more than 600 miles of brutality. He did it to raise money to benefit needy children.

If you envision yourself one day getting yourself to the top of Mount Whitney, it is far from impossible for active people. Assuming that you are in reasonably decent physical condition, here are three considerations:

1. You will need a permit from the Forest Service, available in advance at Lone Pine. Perhaps you have a few friends who would like to accompany you. All need to be named on the permit. Keep in mind that the number of permits issued is limited, so get your request in early.

2. You will have to decide whether you want to go up and down in one day (very difficult), or, like most sane people, take several days. There are places to camp, and you can take your time in the campground to become acclimated to the altitude. At times the camping areas get crowded. The big advantage of going up and down in one day is that you will not have to carry tents, sleeping gear, or multi-day's supply of food. But it is a very rigorous slog up and down.

3. Do you want to do the walk-up route, or the mountaineer's route? My son Chris, who is a fine mountaineer, likes to go up the harder, more interesting way. It is not extremely technical climbing and it avoids the Hundred Switchbacks, which seem to take forever.

A HAWAIIAN ULTRA

The Big Island of Hawaii is, well, *big*. And it supports two very big volcanoes, Mauna Kea and Mauna Loa. Mauna Loa is very active, spewing lava continually down her west flank into the Pacific. Mauna Kea is her gentler, taller sister, home to some of the world's most advanced telescope observatories. At times there is snow atop both of them and tropical skiing is in order above 13,000 feet.

Slicing between the two volcanic massifs is the Saddle Road that runs from the wet side of the Big Island, near Hilo, to the dry side, north of Kailua-Kona. Every year there is a competition among local high schools to run a relay over the Saddle Road from Hilo to Waimea, a distance of 100 kilometers. High school teams consist of ten relay runners, so each participant gets to run ten kilometers. The people who put on the run also invite a small number of ultramarathon runners to do the entire 100 kilometers. In 1995 I had the good fortune to be allowed to participate as an ultramarathon runner.

The thing about this run is that there is only one hill. It starts at sea level in Hilo and goes up and up and up and up, thousands of feet along the Saddle Road. Then it goes down and down and down and down to Waimea. For the first twenty miles or so out of Hilo the road is flanked by lush, tropical vegetation. The flowers are bursting with color, a joy to behold, an inspiration. Above about 5,000 feet the terrain becomes barren and volcanic. Lava boulders lay strewn everywhere, as though the goddess Pele was angry when she formed this land. Beyond the summit you will find ranch land, home to the Parker Ranch, the largest ranch in the USA.

There were not very many ultra runners in our group and I did not feel very competitive. I adopted the Hawaiian strategy of 'hang loose,' take it easy and see what would happen. I can honestly say that I had fun for the first half, with Sylvia crewing for me in a rental car (that was not supposed to be on the Saddle Road.) She drove ahead and stopped every few miles to offer me sustenance. The eerie landscape near the summit was interesting in its own way, and there were great vistas of both Mauna Kea and Mauna Loa to the left and to the right. The hard part came after we started to descend to the dry side. Anyone who thinks that running downhill is easier than running uphill should give the Saddle Road a try. After the first few miles my knees were cussing at me like drunken sailors. Even walking was painful once the knee-knackering had started. It was time for ibuprofen, every half hour until we got to the finish, then a couple more ibuprofen.

The award for ultra runners was a dark green bath towel embroidered in white with the name of the event. I like it better than any of the tee shirts that sit unused in my drawer. I use it after a good tub soak when my aching body needs special tenderness.

A HISTORIC ULTRA: HADRIAN'S WALL

Not all ultra-runs are races. There are places and situations that call upon you to run across a piece of terrain just because it is interesting or beautiful. That is why my friend Mike Banks and I decided to go the full length of Hadrian's Wall in the fall of 1999. The appeal was twofold. It would give me an opportunity to see the north of England up close, and at the same time delve into a piece of history about which I knew very little, the Roman occupation of Britain.

A few decades after the death of Christ the Romans had conquered most of what we now call Britain. When they reached what is approximately the southern border of today's Scotland, they were halted by the wild, blue-painted Picts, ancestors of today's Scots. The first problems seem to have shown up around AD 70 in the vicinity of Solway Firth near where the Scottish-English border meets the Irish Sea. A small contingent of Roman soldiers was rousted by the Picts, who were not interested in becoming a Roman colony. Time after time the Picts upset the expansionist plans of the Romans by raiding their poorly-manned outposts, which were situated far from reinforcements. The Romans were stymied to the point where they just gave up on expanding further north. Somewhere around the end of the second century AD, Emperor Hadrian decided to build a wall clear across northern England to keep the nasty blue people on their own side of the wall. Today the remains of Hadrian's Wall stretch east-west across the far north of England, about 75 miles from the Irish Sea to the North Sea.

Mike Banks and I wanted to traverse the length of Hadrian's Wall, travelling eastward from Bowness-on-Solway to Wall's End, near Newcastle. We set out on a typical drizzly English morning, our first day's goal being to put in about 25 miles. Sylvia and Mike's wife, Pat, had a rental car and were to meet us along the way for lunch, and again at the end of the day's run. We were in no hurry, wanting to visit the small museums along the Wall.

In several places there is little that remains of Hadrian's Wall. Over the centuries the construction stones were removed by local farmers to build farmhouses, sheep cotes, and fences. Our route took us through farmyards, along country roads and at times, along the remnants of the Wall itself. Where the Wall still stands it is either a high earthen berm or a tall, well-built rock construction. In some places the Roman engineers integrated natural rock outcroppings. The remains of stone guard towers are located where they were built, at line-of-sight distances.

Our crossing took us three days. There were no huge climbs, just a lot of minor ups and downs, typical of northern England. The crossing was, in fact, pleasant once the weather cleared up. While Mike and I were moving, our wives went ahead and found us suitable B & B's and pleasant pubs where we could discuss the day's adventures and plan tomorrow's route. The most interesting part of the trip was a small museum in Vindolanda, a former Roman fortress. In that museum the life of a Roman soldier became realistic for me: they were real people, not just ciphers in a book. Among the museum's artifacts were the shoes that the Roman soldiers had actually worn. A letter, inscribed on a wax tablet by a homesick trooper, asks his mother back home to send him some warm socks. The displays also made it clear that the Roman legions were composed of people from many nations, not just from the Italian peninsula, and that some nationalities had military specialties: the Germans were swimmers, used for crossing rivers; the Syrians were skilled at the use of bows and arrows. History takes on an entirely new dimension when you are pursuing it on foot.

Hadrian's Wall finally comes to an end in the northeast of England near Newcastle, where it runs into the North Sea. Even back in Roman times, the Newcastle area was known for its coal deposits. The Romans were good miners, and they dug coal there. From Cornwall, in southern England, they mined and exported metals to other parts of the Roman Empire.

A few miles south of Newcastle you will find Washington Hall, the home of George Washington's forebears. In the town museum you can trace the route taken by the Washington family as they moved from place to place in England, then on to America. In those days the family name was actually 'Wessington', apparently changed for some interesting reasons. Local tales have it that the Wessingtons left the area owing a lot of money.

MORE RECENT HISTORY: THE CHILKOOT TRAIL

"GOLD! GOLD!" They shouted when the first gold-laden ships landed in Seattle with news of the 1896 Klondike gold strike. Times were tough in America, with high unemployment and men willing to go far afield to support their families. (Does that sound familiar?) The possibility of striking it rich drew thousands from all over the United States, and from as far away as Europe and Australia. They begged, borrowed and, sometimes, stole enough money to get them there and to furnish a grubstake, pick and shovel in hand. Most of them had no idea of what they were getting into, but they stampeded on, relying on sheer guts and hoping against all odds for good luck.

The first and biggest problem would be getting to the place where they could find that alluring yellow stuff. It was in the northwest of Canada, extremely distant from almost any other place. There were three ways that a 'stampeder' could make the trip. The first would be to undertake an extremely rigorous and dangerous journey of thousands of miles on foot or horseback across the bulk of the Canadian wilderness. There were no roads, and most of the territory had not yet been explored or mapped. The second route required going by ship, around Cape Horn and via Seattle, northward in the Pacific to the mouth of the Yukon River, then all the way up the Yukon River towards its source in Canada. The third and best way of getting there was to catch a ship from Seattle to Skagway, Alaska, then walk across the Chilkoot Trail to the Yukon. ("Seward's Folly," Alaska, had been purchased from Russia a few decades before.) None of these routes was easy. And while the first two were almost impossible, considering the huge distances, the remoteness and northern climatic conditions, an extremely small number of hardy souls did succeed. The majority of the prospectors opted for the Seattle-Skagway-Yukon route.

It is important to note that the border between Canada and the US Territory of Alaska had not yet been firmly agreed upon. With the prospect of thousands of American miners crossing into Canada, the Canadian government swiftly and wisely made a decision and arbitrarily settled the matter of where the border was. They dispatched a company of Mounties to control the pass that the miners would have to use to enter Canada. The Mounties made it clear that anyone crossing that pass would be in British Columbia, Canada. Because they did not want thousands of penniless settlers bringing their problems to Canada, they set a requirement that each settler had to bring what amounted to two tons of provisions, enough to last through a cold Yukon winter. This put a literally very heavy burden on the prospectors: they would have to haul all of that food and equipment across the mountains, either on their backs, or on horseback, or on the backs of local Indians who would charge an exorbitant price for their services. Many of them turned back home in discouragement, not just because of the costs, but also because of the extreme physical difficulty of carrying two tons of goods across wild and rugged country. A man named Henry De Windt said in 1897, *"The trail is difficult, and dangerous to those who are not possessed of steady nerve."* In more recent times, the superintendent of the Klondike Gold Rush Historical Park is quoted as saying, *"The steep climb from the Scales to the summit of the pass is extremely intimidating … wet, cold and windy conditions, combined with the exhausting climb up the steep snow and boulder slope is a major challenge."* Still, many of the gold seekers would not be dissuaded. Unfortunately, by the time most of them got to the goldfields all of the worthwhile plots had already been staked out. The people who made the biggest fortunes in the Gold Rush were the people in Seattle and Skagway who gouged the prospectors for overpriced provisions, and the prostitutes, barkeeps and thieves who preyed on the few miners who were lucky to come up with a few nuggets of gold.

Crossing the Chilkoot Trail sounded like fun to Mike and me. "We really have to do that!" said Mike in an email from his home in England. We arrived in Skagway on August 6, 2001 and took a room at the historic Golden North Hotel. In my dreams that night I imagined that I heard the lovely ladies of the evening whispering sweet nothings to the gullible miners as the barkeep slipped a Mickey Finn into their drinks. Soon enough Mike and I were awake and ready to get on with our quest.

Trail permits and topographic maps in hand, the next morning we hitched a ride to nearby Dyea, the trailhead for the Chilkoot Trail. The Trail covers more than 50 kilometers of rough back country, including one extremely steep climb from the Scales to the Summit. Once you leave Dyea you are in a heavily forested wilderness, moving beneath towering evergreens. You will not find a restaurant, a shop or any other sign of civilization anyplace along the Trail. The first 13 miles are relatively flat, following the lower part of the Dyea River to your left, far below you. The music of the river combined with the smell of forest and moist earth gave me a feeling of euphoria. The bright early sun pushed its way through the trees in mottled patches. It was a breathtaking time and place to be alive. But it is in this area where many bear encounters take place, with lots of both grizzlies and black bears. We wore bear bells and saw only a couple of beavers and a large bull moose, water dribbling profusely down his nose as he filched greens from the riverbed. After mile 13 the trail starts to rise, first gradually, then sharply. At mile 16 you hit

The Scales, the place where miners had to put down their belongings as they prepared for the long, hard hump up to the Summit. When the Park Superintendent says 'steep,' you may read 'extremely steep,' even vertical, and that is no exaggeration. The trip from the Scales up to the Summit is only a half mile horizontally, but it entails hundreds of feet of elevation gain in a very short distance, climbing a trail that would be more suitable for mountain goats, strewn with boulders and the bones of pack animals that gave up their spirits here. It is almost a cliff. The area is prone to falling rocks, so it is not a good idea to be too close behind the person in front of you.

It took us over an hour to reach the Summit from the Scales. We had reached Canada! When we stopped at the Summit for a drink of water and some trail mix there were no Mounties to welcome us into Canada or to check that we had brought the two tons of provisions that the prospectors were required to haul. The view from the top was awe inspiring. We could look back and see across the treetops all the way to the sea at Dyea, where we had started, far to the west. Modern license plates in Alaska show the famous picture of a long, bleak line of dreary but hopeful stampeders slowly trudging their weary way up the slope, shouldering their heavy burdens, step by perilous step, up to the Summit. We signed the register book at the top and continued on, now going gradually downhill, passing Morrow Lake and Deep Lake. This part of the Trail was easy going, but not always obvious. The miners camped here and cut down almost all of the trees along the lakes to build boats to carry them downstream the rest of the way to the Yukon gold fields. Even here. they were still far from their destination. There are reminders of their lakeside camps strewn about, rusted fry pans, stoves and the occasional grave. On we went with an increased appreciation of what those rugged individuals had gone through a century ago.

Our goal was to catch the day's last train on the White Pass Railway at the end of Lindeman Lake, to take us back to Skagway and our warm hotel beds. We made it with just minutes to spare, tired and very happy. Mike would go home to England with tales of the wild frontier and I would plan our next adventure, which would be in Tasmania, Australia.

THE OVERLAND TREK, TASMANIA

Sometimes you get really, really lucky. For five years I had a job writing a monthly column for a British magazine with the second largest circulation in Britain (second to Reader's Digest). My columns covered two general areas of interest, (1) what was going on in America and (2) writing about my adventures. I really liked the adventure part of it because my editors would send me someplace like the Chilkoot Trail or Hadrian's Wall. They would pay my travel expenses, then they would pay me to write about it. *What a great job that was!*

The editor asked me what I thought about the Tasmanian tiger (also called the Tasmanian wolf), a carnivorous Australian marsupial that has been extinct since the year of my birth. The last Tasmanian tiger had died in a zoo that long ago, I told him. "But," he said, "there are still occasional reports coming in from people in wild Tasmania claiming to have spotted a live Tasmanian tiger." Most people scoff at those reports, ascribing them to the guilty conscience of a nation that needlessly eradicated the relatively harmless buggers from the face of the earth. Still, my editor suggested, "Wouldn't it be nice if you and Mike Banks did a foray down into the Tasmanian outback to see if there just might be a few of those wee beasties lurking someplace in the outback?"

Are you kidding? A trip to Australia? To have fun in the woods? I hesitated for about a quarter of a millisecond, not wanting to sound too enthusiastic. Two weeks later photographer Mike Banks and I met in Launceston, Tasmania, the southernmost state in Australia. We had two weeks to look for the tiger. On the slim chance that one or more might have survived, it could be hiding anywhere in that entire island state. Our plan was to go the second most remote part of the state and cross it looking for our quarry. (This is not about a long run, but I thought you might enjoy hearing about it anyway.)

Mike and I were on an expense account, so we hired a guide who knew the area intimately, who would cook for us and set up our tents. He even packed in wine. You can't really search for deviously hiding beasts when you are tied up with all of those mundane chores, can you?

FLASHBACK: Mike and I have been hiking for three days on the Overland Trek, a trail that goes through one of the wildest parts of Tasmania, which is the wildest state in all of Australia. We have seen a lot of beasts, all marsupials. Our guide's name is Jake. He calls everyone else "Mate," probably because Jake can't remember anyone else's name. But Jake is the real McCoy. There is not much that he does not know about the outback.

There is no shortage of barrel-like wombats, the marsupial equivalent of burrowing pigs. I always thought that a kangaroo was just a kangaroo, but I have seen so many variations of 'roos that I have lost count. To keep it simple, our guide says, "Just divide them into two groups: the kangaroos and the wallabies. The 'roos are generally bigger, like the big reds and grays, except for the ones that are smaller, like the tree roos that are more like rats. The wallabies are smaller, except for …"

"Enough of that," Mike tells him," we are here to look for Tasmanian tigers." Jake is upset. "Mate, ain't no one seen none a them in years. They ain't 'ere no more, Mate. They're long gone, Mate." To keep us happy Jake takes us on a night hike (after we polish off two bottles of good wine.) We halt and he shushes us as he cocks an ear, hearing something that we can't hear. "Foller me, and be real quiet." After pushing

115

through the bush for a few minutes, Jake shines his flashlight into the beady, glaring red eyes of a Tasmanian devil. The devil is a smaller marsupial carnivore, much smaller than the Tiger. But this is the closest we will get to seeing his elusive bigger cousin.

We finally did spot two Tasmanian tigers. One was the last of its species, his stuffed, mangy remains relegated to a museum in Launceston for about 70 years. The poor dog-like critter looked more dusty than scary. The other Tasmanian tiger was on the label of a can of excellent beer. Tasmania brews two of the best beers in all of Australia, a country that appreciates beer. One brand is Cascade, and the other is Boag's. The only way to decide which is best is to sit down and make a slow comparison. It will take several pints of each before you reach a conclusion. Then you can tell everyone about how, one dark and lonely night, you came across a ferocious Tasmanian tiger on the trail Down Under, the last of its breed.

BIG GUYS CAN RUN, TOO

When people think about distance runners, the stereotype that comes to mind is the 135 pound runner, like Frank Shorter or Bill Rodgers. They, of course, are our representatives at the Olympics, and they clock mile after mile in the sub-five minute range. But big guys can run long distances, too. They might not be as fast, but pound for pound those competing in the Clydesdale division are just as athletic and heroic as the Olympians. Two come to mind immediately.

Colonel Buck Swannock, USMC, Retired, was one of my heroes. You do not get to be a colonel in the Marines by being a pussycat. Buck was willing to try almost anything, and quite often could be found on his way to earth under a parachute. When he was running marathons, it would be wise to not be too close: he took up room, both physically and psychically. One of my most prized possessions is a silver port cup that Buck gave me, a Marine Corps memento.

Larry Gibbs was a top notch basketball player at Bradley U in the tough mid-west college league. When I knew him in California he had bulked up somewhat. That is when he started to put himself through the grind in long distance running races. During one of the Western States 100 runs (was it 1983?) he ran into some trouble at around the 70 mile mark. I was one of his support crew, and we became concerned when he did not show up at a check point. When we found him, he was exhausted, horizontal on a medical cot, wanting to die. Remembering that it was his birthday, I presented him with a greasy doughnut topped with a candle. That was enough to get him off his butt to finish the 100 miler.

WOMEN IN ULTRAMARATHONS

I would be remiss if I did not mention that women have shown a remarkable aptitude for competing in ultramarathons. Among the best in my era were Sally Edwards and Skip Swannock. Keeping in mind that I come from an earlier (troglodyte) era, on behalf of myself and my contemporaries I ask their forbearance and offer them encouragement and congratulations for overcoming unnecessary hurdles. I am sure that the reader has noticed that there are more women than men running and jogging along the roads lately.

A FEW WORDS ABOUT ULTRAS

Like Baskin-Robbins ice cream, ultra running events come in many flavors, but your two primary approaches are to either enter a well-organized event like the Western States 100 (or maybe an ill-organized non-event like one of the ubiquitous Fat-Ass-Fifty runs.). Alternatively, you can put on your own do-it-yourself ultra run. I like both approaches, but I am a sucker for the challenge of inventing my own fun and in the game of survival.

Pick up any map and pore over it for a while. Geological Survey maps are good, and you will find a plethora of good maps on the Internet or at any REI shop. Even a AAA road map might suffice for some projects. (Note that you can locate access points to the Appalachian Trail or the Pacific Coast Trail on most state AAA maps.) Select a couple of points in an area that interests you, especially if the countryside in between is noteworthy. Then think about what it would take for you to run from point A to point B. If you think that it is within your capabilities, then put together a plan for your run, whether it is a run of an hour, a marathon or a multiday run. It is best if you have a buddy with you, and make sure that you have planned for everything that you might need, including food and clothing, maybe shelter. Think also about permits, finances and how you will handle emergencies. Will there be dangerous animals like cougars and grizzlies? Consider the effects of a long absence on your family, job and school. When you are satisfied that you have a good plan and are properly prepared, share your plan with a few trusted friends and get their opinions, then go for it.

Here is an example of a really difficult quest that someone might try. In November of 1970 a man who came to be known as D. B. Cooper skyjacked a Northwest Orient flight going from Portland, Oregon to Seattle. Cooper showed a crew member a bomb in his briefcase. In return for freeing the passengers and most of the crew in Seattle, Cooper demanded parachutes and a sack filled with $200,000 in ransom money. Shortly after the plane left Seattle, he parachuted from the plane into the deeply forested area between Seattle and Portland. It was a dark night and there was a raging winter storm. The FBI thinks that he may have died during his jump, but no one knows or is talking about it. A few years later some of the money showed up not far from where he jumped. There is a lot of rough terrain between Seattle and Portland, but the flight path and the cash that later turned up give some pretty good clues to where a runner might come across the briefcase (loaded with dynamite), the remains of the parachute, what is left of the cash, or maybe even D.B Cooper's earthly remains. It would take a lot of bushwhacking, but the search would be an interesting challenge and a great deal of fun, even if you find nothing.

Or you might run all the way down from the South Rim of the Grand Canyon to the bottom, then up to the North Rim. When you get to the top, turn around and run back. It is one hell of a challenge. If you are thinking about it, remember that water will be a very big problem, so you will have to carry a lot of it. Keep in mind, too, that there is a large change in altitude. At the bottom it can be very hot and on the same day it will be quite cold as you get close to the top. When my son Chris was a student at the University of Arizona in Tucson, he took a trip to the Grand Canyon, up and down from the South Rim. Everything was peachy on the way down and most of the way back up. Then the temperature started to drop, and he was becoming hypothermic. If you are interested in this journey, I urge you to talk to the rangers for advice and to file a plan on your proposed itinerary. That way they will be able to start the search for your body before the crows finish picking at your bones.

Set your goals and think big. Make it something worth working hard to plan and execute. But make sure that your goal is in line with what you can reasonably expect from your body. Opportunities are all around you if you just open your eyes to them. You might find D. B. Cooper's loot. You could create a challenge that no one has ever attempted, maybe even your own 'first ascent', maybe even a Guinness listing. Why not?

Now where did I put those topo maps?

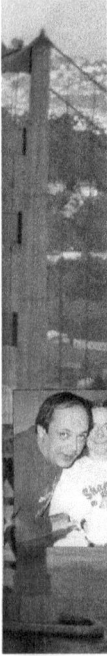

Fat Ass Fifty

Keine Anmeldegebühr, keine Verpflegungsstation, keine Siegerehrung – so oder ähnlich lesen sich die Ankündigungen zu den »Recover from the Holidays Fat Ass Fifty« (wörtlich übersetzt: Erholung von den Feiertagen Fetter Arsch Fünfzig) Läufen, die um den Jahreswechsel herum, überall in Nordamerika stattfinden. Um jegliche Mißverständnisse zu vermeiden, fügen besonders besorgte Veranstalter noch hinzu: »no wimps« – »keine Weichlinge«.

Von rechts: Joe Oaks, Begründer der Fat Ass 50 Tradition; Jos Walle, Gründer des Toronto, Kanada, Fat Ass 50; Velo Petrovskis, Joe's friend aus Estonia

The Fat Ass Fifty went international. This article is from a German Magazine.

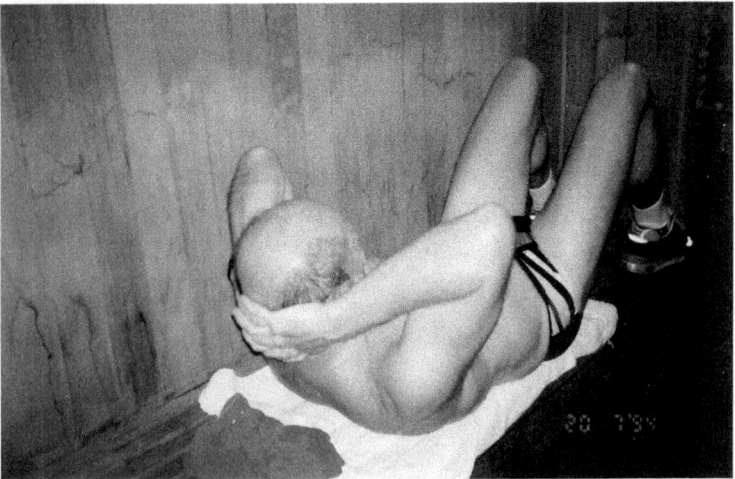

I trained for the 1994 Badwater/Death Valley run by doing 1,000 sit-ups a day in a 150 F sauna.

120

Death Valley. I am with Marat "The Camel" Zhilanbaev from Kazakhstan at Badwater.

Badwater: I wore an Arab outfit for the intense heat.

Badwater: The long, long, long road up to Whitney Portal.

Badwater: After Whitney Portal you still have to run the 100 switchbacks and a lot more.

Badwater: On top of Mount Whitney. Death Valley is in the far distance behind me.

Four Corners run: We were finally stopped by the snow above Whitney Portal.

Four Corners run: Feodor Sklokin, Vitaly Kornovsky; Marat Zhilanbaev; Joe Oakes; Doctor Ben Jones; Denise Jones; Feodor and Vitaly were the support crew. Doctor Jones is the "Mayor of Badwater." This was shortly after Marat's very interesting exposure to a Nevada brothel.

The temperature at the start of the Badwater race was 120 F on Ben Jones thermometer. Badwater is the lowest place in the Western Hemisphere at 282 feet below sea level.

Alaska remembers the Chilkoot Trail on its license plates.

Hadrian's Wall is a small version of the Great Wall of China, both built to keep invaders away.

The Romans built Hadrian's Wall to keep the pesky Picts out. Mike and I at a craggy spot on the Wall. Scotland is in the distance to the north.

Running along Hadrian's Wall is not easy. It is 70+ miles of hills, all uphill.

And Then There Were Super-Marathons

"Grace strikes us when we are in great pain …….. Sometimes at that moment a wave of light breaks into our darkness…"
  – *Paul Johannes Tillich*

"Hard pounding, gentlemen; but we shall see who can pound the longest."
  – *Wellington at Waterloo*

"A journey of a thousand miles must begin with a single step."
  – *Lao Tzu*

A running journey of 1,000 miles? Why not? I was at a Sri Chinmoy ultra-marathon run in Flushing Meadows, New York several years ago, at the old World's Fair site. One of the distances being contested was, in fact, 1,000 miles, and several of the great Sri Chinmoy's followers were competing at that distance. I said to myself, "That is an extraordinarily long distance to run." Then I thought about the fact that when your ancestors and mine travelled out of Africa to populate the rest of the world, they moved far greater distances than 1,000 miles, and they did it one step at a time. No one knows what a typical day's journey might have been for them, but added together those daily journeys brought us all of us around the globe. They put one foot in front of the other and kept moving. A modern super-marathon is like that: You do today's journey, you rest; then you get up and do it again tomorrow, and again the next day. Alcoholics Anonymous' motto is 'One day at a time.' Let's rephrase that for the super-marathon runners: 'One marathon at a time: every day.'"

CHAPTER SEVEN
AND THEN THERE WERE SUPER-MARATHONS

SUPER-MARATHONS

A few words about Hard Core runners: During the Running Boom of the 1970s a 'Hard Core' runner was someone who trained for and ran marathons. The Hard Cores went forth and multiplied to the point where, after a few years, tens of thousands of them were participating in large scale marathons like New York, London, Los Angeles and Chicago, with thousands of participants. Suddenly marathon runners were no longer very special. In the 1980s the ante was upped for becoming a 'Hard Core' runner: 26 miles was no longer enough. The Hardest of the Hard Core marathoners transformed themselves into ultra-marathoners. It was predictable that soon enough we started seeing fields of hundreds in ultramarathon events such as the Western States 100 Miler and the JFK 50, and the best races filled up fast. Came the nineties, folks, and ultras were no longer the ticket to the ultimate in Hard Core. The buzz word became 'super-marathon'. Sorry, Ultra Guys, move up or step out.

What is it that makes a *super-marathon* different from an *ultra-marathon*? An *ultra-marathon* is any continuous running event that is longer than the standard marathon distance of 26 miles, 385 yards; A *super-marathon* is a *series* of several standard marathons. It is contested over a number of successive days, usually between seven and fourteen days. These daily marathons are often linked end-to-end. They cover a large swath of ground, sometimes in an interesting geographic, cultural or historic area. The format will vary from event to event, but the daily distance is a full marathon, more or less. I say 'more or less' because, even though the stages are all approximately marathon distances, the daily starting and finishing points might be determined by the location of a feature such as a castle or a village center, not by a precisely measured distance. I have been involved in several super-marathons. There have not been many overall because of the enormous logistics involved. A race director has to be *really, really* dedicated. If making money is his objective, he might be better off slinging hamburgers.

TRANS-SIBERIA SUPERMARATHON

This was my first super-marathon experience, and it was a whopper. It took place during late years of the Soviet Union, and we ran across a very big piece of Siberia. Much of it was along a railway right of way, the *Baikal-Amur Magistral*. Every morning we would eat a small breakfast and run from one village to the next. When we got to the day's destination we would be welcomed by the local Communist Party chief, given a meal and offered beds at what can best be described as the local political version of a Boy/Girl Scouts camp, known in Russia as Pioneers. The next morning we would do the same thing, and the next, and the next, and the next, ad infinitum. The organizer was not the nicest guy in the world, and unknown to us, he had us travelling illegally in restricted areas where foreigners were not supposed to be. But you know what? We had a very interesting time, and by crossing Siberia on foot we did what no other running group in history had been able to do.

FLASHBACK: We are in Irkutsk, Siberia, USSR, several time zones to the east of Moscow. The Trans-Siberia Super-marathon is finally over. We are waiting for the organizers (whom we have come to call The Pinocchio Gang because of all the lies they have been telling us) to arrange our flight back to Moscow. From Moscow we can catch our reserved flight to JFK. They have all of us cramped into a tiny, dirty apartment. Pinocchio Sr. says he is doing us a favor by sending 'ladies' to the room to entertain us, and one of our younger runners seems to have fallen in love. Pinocchio sends a couple of sleazy characters to the room to try to buy our clothing. Western style clothing is simply not available in the USSR. Watch your wallets!

But today we have another problem. Ted Epstein, a runner from Colorado, has gone missing. That is unlike Ted. He is a mature professional, very dependable. Before we can come up with a search plan, in comes Ted. He has been out running. He tells us that he felt that running across Siberia was not enough mileage for him, so he was out logging even more miles. Ted tells me privately that he is not going to wait for Pinocchio to arrange for our flight to Moscow: During his run he visited a synagogue and met a person who will help him to get a flight to Moscow.

Pinocchio Junior comes into the room, beaming his big phony grin. "My dear friends, I have good news for you. Tomorrow morning we will be leaving Irkutsk. I have arranged for a flight to beautiful Kiev in the Ukraine." Kiev is his home. He does not tell us why we are going there instead of Moscow, but it is pretty clear. In Moscow he would be questioned by the KGB for some of his activities in Siberia. In Kiev he will be safe: he knows whom to bribe.

It is a long story, going from funny to ludicrous, too long to be told here. If you are interested, I have included a full chapter about running across Siberia in my book, *With a Single Step*, the story of my non-motorized circumnavigation of the earth.

The Trans-Siberia Super-marathon was held just once, thank God.

ZOLOTAYA KALTSO

Zolotaya Kaltso is Russian for Golden Circle. It refers to a circle of ancient Russian cities, living museums, about 200 kilometers northeast of Moscow, each of which is known for its magnificent golden domed churches. This is the historic heart of Russian Orthodoxy. Several years ago I was asked by my friend, Gennady Schvets, the leading sports journalist in the USSR, to organize an American team to run in the July 1990 Golden Circle Super-Marathon. After a lot of phone calls we put together a solid team of hard-core, experienced *ultra*-marathon runners, but none of them had ever run a super-marathon. On the team were Gary Hill from Nebraska, Bill and Bea Beddor from Minnesota, Canadians Esmond Mah and Jo Welles, Mike Modzelewski, who lives in Florida, New Yorker Dick Opsahl, John Warren, Tom Ziola and Ed Kelley from California. The Hawaiian Ultra-Running Team (HURT) gave us John and P.J. Salmonson and Jim Budde. Rounding out the team were New Jersey's Paul Soyka and myself. Our team looked strong, and we were especially blessed by the two gifted Canadians. Jo Wells has run the full distance across Canada, and Esmond is the nephew of marathon legend Sy Mah, who held the world record for the most marathons runs. The schedule called for ten marathons in ten days for a total of 262 miles, although the over-zealous Russians billed it as 500 kilometers.

Three teams were in contention for the team prize: A very strong team of Russians; a western European team put together by Francois Faure from Brittany, France; and our gang of North Americans, who were almost all over 40. Because of some problems that I do not remember, Russia's Aeroflot got us to Moscow too late for the scheduled race start. The Russians were kind enough to delay the race for a day for us. The official race starter was the 10 km gold medal winner from the 1960 Rome Olympics, Pyotr Bolotnikov, who had at one time held the world and Olympic records for 10,000 meters. Also in official attendance was the stunning and very approachable current Mrs. USSR, whose presence lent the race Dolly Parton-like dimensions rarely found at running events.

The race started with a big bang, literally. Because the organizers could not find a starting pistol, (this was the USSR, after all) Pyotr Bolotnikov was given a flare gun to start the race. Now good old Pyotr, who was sober at the time, was not familiar with this fancy piece of equipment, and reasoning that if he aimed the gun skyward the flare might fall to the ground and burn down the village, he aimed it instead toward the ground. When he pulled the trigger, the burning phosphorous flare ricocheted off the ground right into the gut of startled American runner Dick Opsahl. The impact knocked Dick on his bum and the flare burned the skin on his belly. Being of sturdy Viking stock, Opsahl got up and ran after the others, who were now about 50 yards ahead. The only one who stayed back to help Opsahl up was the token Dutchman, Ger Wijenberg.

The French team doctor was appalled by all of this. The good doctor, however, was mollified by being given the opportunity to accompany the multidimensional Mrs. USSR throughout the race. Being a Frenchman and a chivalrous type (and away from home), he accepted with gusto. Unfortunately, he allowed Mrs. USSR to drive his medical vehicle, the only auto we had following the race. That way the doctor could keep his eyes on Mrs. USSR instead of the road. What *M le Docteur* did not know was that the voluptuous Mrs. USSR, like most Russians in those days, had never driven an automobile. Within minutes she drove the car into a very large tree, giving M le Docteur a whiplash that required a neck brace for the rest of his time in Russia. If he bore any other-than-chivalrous intentions regarding the usage of Mrs. USSR, his hopes were, sadly, dashed.

Every day we ran a marathon from one golden-onion-domed city to the next golden-onion-domed city: Vladimir, Suzdal, Zolotnikova Pustyn, Ivanovo, Privolysk, Volgaveschensk, Kostroma, Mali Solye, Yaroslavl, Rostov the Great, Davidovo and Uglich, all beautiful cities steeped in the richness of ancient Russian Orthodox culture and history. Between the cities we ran through agricultural land, tilled for centuries by the same families. This country, this soil, was in their blood, and much of their blood had been spilled for it. Russians are spiritually tied to the land. The word that they use for it is *narodnaya*, a concept that we wandering Americans find hard to fully understand.

This was Communist Russia, and each day we were officially the guests of the local Communist Party in every town we visited. Russians love to throw a party, especially at the Party's expense, and our presence gave them their excuse. To celebrate each day's marathon and to entertain their guests, there was always a big evening affair for us to attend. If you have ever run a marathon, or are planning to run one tomorrow, (or both) you know that you do not really *want* to party every night. Not wanting to seem ungracious and spoil their fun, we decided that every Communist Party party would be attended by a token one or two of us. Our daily human sacrificial runner/guest was chosen daily by lottery.

FLASHBACK: We have arrived in the city of Kostroma and it is my turn in the barrel as the sacrificial American marathoner. The French team has cruelly donated their injured doctor. At the end of the morning's marathon the doctor and I are taken to a luxurious compound outside the city, a place reserved for Communist Party elite. First on the agenda is a sauna ('banya' in Russian), where we are each given liter bottles of "good Russian beer" called "pivo." "Drink pivo and sweat, Joseph. Is good," advises our host. In truth Russian beer tastes like something that just came out of a horse. We roast and rest for a while before being called for late afternoon dinner, but it is a long time before we actually get to the food. As with all Russian celebrations, ours starts with several rounds of toasts by our Communist Party hosts, counter-toasts by the doctor and me, in Russian, French and English. Language makes little difference because Russian toasts are made with tumblers full of vodka and after the first toast one might as well have been speaking Martian and reciting nursery rhymes for all anyone gives a damn. Toasting seems to be a way of saying, "Let's have another drink." Finally the food comes.

I am sure that it is an excellent meal, but my brain cells were too soaked in alcohol to remember any of it. I can tell you that the food was accompanied by copious quantities of good Soviet champagne from Azer-baijan. Then, after the second round of after-dinner Georgian cognac toasts, I excused myself and literally fell face-forward out the door, los-ing my dinner as I plunged into a dark void. At that moment all went blank. In the morning I woke up looking at the French doctor, who was sleeping in bed next to me, snoring like a walrus until I woke him with a scream. I do not know who was more horrified, he or I.

It is morning and I deserve this, the mother-of-all-hangovers.. Mea culpa, oh my head! Before starting the days marathon I try every cure in the books simultaneously, Russian, French and American. Breakfast is a handful of aspirin tablets. Then I start running the day's marathon with the others. The first mile is dreadful, with several bush stops. But the pain has slowly become just numbness and bad memories. I run on, confident in the fact that tonight it will be someone else's turn in the bar-rel playing the part of the good American diplomat.

Between the Golden Circle cities we ran through farmland and small villages. For the most part we were on dusty country roads, not much paved. A feeling of nostalgia comes into my mind: *Gary Hill, Bill Beddor and I are slowly running together past a farmhouse. We are far back in the race, with no other runners in sight. In the distance we hear music, and as we get close we see a smiling, toothless old man with a droopy mustache looking down from his hayloft, pumping away at his accordion for us. Below him a babushka (grandmother) energetically cranks the hand pump to offer us a drink of her delicious well water. Our feet grow lighter. Our pace picks up. Maybe we are in a runner's version of Fiddler on the Roof.*

We encountered one problem that you will never find in Amer-ican marathons: The Russian Air Force. This consists of massive swarms of mosquitoes (the fighter planes), accompanied by huge deer flies (the dive bombers). Gary Hill from Nebraska said that the reason that there were no snakes or spiders is that the flies ate them all. He described them as "having the appetite of a runner with the teeth of a great white shark."

One member of the Russian team was forty-something Russian Army General Evgeniy Kornienko, who was followed by a jeep-load of his troops to cheer him on as he ran. He set an example that his men, half his age, would have trouble duplicating. A few years later I saw the general on TV, promoted to be the military attache to the Russian Ambassador to the UN.

In the evenings those of us who were not on sacrificial duty would come together to eat and go over the day's results. The Russians always dusted the competition. The Americans and Europeans were happy to just finish one more in a series of marathons. Sometimes we sang songs, like rounds of Frere Jaques with various teams singing in French, Russian or English. We told jokes, some quite difficult to translate. The Russian runners tried hard to be friendly hosts and to entertain us. Russians love music and I believe that there are more guitar players in Russia than anywhere. The French runners, as individuals, were okay, but always seemed to have a chip on their shoulders.

The top ten places went to Russians. Lev Hitterman was first overall with a total time of 28 hours 36 minutes for the ten marathons, averaging below 2:50 per marathon, day after day. Lev later confided in me that he was a Jew, a small minority in Russia. "In Russia my internal passport says that I am a Jew, not a Russian. Jews cannot ever have 'Russian' on their passports. That is just the way it is, even though my family has been here hundreds of years." We saw an example of extreme Russian ultra-nationalism when we went to an evening concert in a city park. Tom Ziola (who is Polish-American) was attacked by a man who just disliked the idea that we were foreigners attending a free concert in a park in his home town. The police subdued him, but there was no legal follow-up.

Following the race we were returned to Moscow via a three day cruise on a steel barge. Did I say cruise? It was rustic at best. There was only one tiny sleeping compartment, and that became Mrs. USSR's bed chamber. The rest of us slept in the open, on a cold steel deck without bedrolls and only a few thin blankets. And guess what: it was drizzling. Somehow the Russians forgot to bring food *(What a surprise!)*, except for a few loaves of tasty black bread and a lot of vodka, so we scrounged what we could in canal-side villages that had little to share. In one town we managed to buy a single duck and barbecued it on an open fire on the steel deck, to be shared among about 20 of us. I was the hero of the day. Having traveled in Russia before, I knew that food would probably be a problem: Inside my pack was a three pound jar of peanut butter and two dozen energy bars. Dinner was peanut butter on black bread, a tiny piece of charred *duck ala canal*, half of a Power Bar and lots of vodka to wash it down. It was not *haute cuisine*, but even the snooty Frenchmen went at it with gusto.

LA GRANDE COURSE DE BRETAGNE

Brittany, *Bretagne*, is located on the west coast of France, about midway between the border with Spain on the south and Belgium on the north, flanked north and south by the English Channel and the tumultuous Bay of Biscay. It juts out into the frigid Atlantic, like Charles de Gaulle's nose, sitting just south of the flat bottom of Britain. To be a Breton is to be aquatic. The Bretons, surrounded by the sea, are great fishermen, and they know how to prepare seafood exquisitely, with world renowned local oysters their specialty. The 1944 WWII D Day invasion took place in Normandy, just north of Brittany. Our group of runners was enacting our own invasion of Brittany 48 years later in the form of a super-marathon.

The French do things their own way, and it can be wonderful. In May, 1992 Mssr. Francois Faure put together a super-marathon that he called *La Grande Course de Bretagne*, The Grand Course of Brittany. Let me first explain that Brittany is technically part of France, and while the Bretons do not deny being French, they claim a heritage that is quite distinct from their countrymen. Culturally and ethnically the Bretons are a Celtic people, and that heritage is reflected in every aspect of their lives. When they celebrate, they play bagpipes and wear kilts. It would be difficult for a Parisian to hold a conversation with a Breton because the local *patois* is more closely related to the Welsh language, unrelated to French. Parisians and do not understand a word of the Breton language.

M Faure, founder of the club *les Marathoniens de l'Aventure* (Marathon Adventurers) put together a wonderful race. He invited runners from all over the world. He asked me to organize an American team. Our team included Tom Possert, Gary Hill, John Surdyk, Noelle Relyea, Dick Opsahl, Jonathan Lovy, Debra Moore, Jo Welles, Gary Hill, Andrew Lovy, Stan Hardesty and myself. Other runners came from Russia, France, Czechoslovakia, Hungary, Poland, Finland, Canada, England, Iran and Holland. We were housed in hostels, schools and private homes, and the food was superb. But of course it would be, we were in France, weren't we?

The start of the race was in the most spectacular place I have ever seen for a race start. The magnificent castle at Mont St. Michel looms up from the sea about a half mile out in the bay of the same name. Beyond the bay is Atlantic Ocean and the English Channel. The castle is tied to the mainland by a narrow causeway that is under water during high spring tides. When the tide ebbs the causeway is passable, with broad mud flats on both sides. It was at Mont St. Michel that we gathered for our super-marathon start.

This super-marathon differed from others in that each day's marathon was broken into two half marathons: one in the morning and the other in the afternoon. Each day we started with an early communal *petite dejeuner*, a breakfast of bread, pastries and coffee. Faure's formula had us running each morning's 21-kilometer half marathon into a Breton village where the mayor and the townsfolk enthusiastically awaited us. It was a day of celebration for the villagers, having all these foreign runners right in their own town. There were speeches, awards presentations and a fine French mid-day meal. After lunch we were given a chance to nap before the day's second half marathon took us to another village, where another mayor and another enthusiastic crowd greeted us like returning war heroes. We ended running stages in Fougeres, Parc d'Armorique, Huelgoat, Landelau, Rohan, Saint Jean Brevaly, Redon, Bruc sur Aff, 19 towns in all, linked together by 18 races in nine days. In each of these places the local populace welcomed us with food, a place to sleep and an evening of entertainment. The most enjoyable part of it was staying with local families and getting to know the hospitable Bretons. I have heard some American tourists complain about the French, but we super-marathon runners were treated like dear friends.

Our daily runs took us through picture-postcard farmland, forests, old villages, and along miles of tree lined barge canals that were built by Napoleon centuries ago. Brittany is sparsely populated, so for the most part our route was blissfully quiet. We were in dreamland.

FLASHBACK: I am running under a canopy of old trees along one of Napoleon's canals in the middle of Brittany. The stately shade trees are centuries old. I can see Jo Welles about 200 meters in front of me, otherwise I am alone enjoying the solitude. There is no barge traffic on the ancient canal, and there are no automobiles on the narrow road that parallels it. The sun pierces through breaks in the branches, mottling the ground with an irregular pattern of splashes of sunlight. I want to sing out loud because it is it is such a beautiful place to be alive and to be running. And everywhere, even here the middle of nowhere, when we come across local people, they greet us courteously. The farmers and fishermen seem to know who we are and they are pleased that we have come to run in their small corner of Brittany.

The runners at the front, as always, were killing themselves trying to put up good race times day after day. Most willing to self-destruct were the Russians and the Eastern Europeans. I suspect that the Hungarians, Czechs and Poles wanted desperately to stick it to their Russian oppressors. But the Russians were there to compete and determined to win, despite having travelled for three days in a cramped bus from Moscow, arriving late the night before the start. The final results would have made the United Nations proud. The top ten runners were from Russia, Czechoslovakia, Poland, Hungary, Great Britain (by way of Iran), Finland, France, and the USA. Our top runner, Ohioan Tom Possert, is one of the best super-marathoners the USA has ever produced.

After the *Grande Tour de Bretagne* we wearily and happily went our separate ways. My way took me to Russia to continue on the next leg of my non-motorized circumnavigation of the earth.

AND MORE SUPERMARATHONS ....

After the Grande Course de Bretagne, Tomas Rusek, the great Czech runner, invited me to bring an American team to run a super-marathon that went from castle to castle in the Moravian region of what was then Czechoslovakia, now the Czech Republic. Alas, the timing was not right and we did not go. What I heard later was that it was a superb event, run in an atmosphere that brought the runners centuries back into Eastern European history.

Perhaps the super-marathon that has gotten the most hype in the running press is *Le Marathon des Sables*, in the Sahara. It is produced by a French group. Runners are required to carry packs containing their food, water, bedding and a list of required items as they run across the desert day after day. John Warren ran it several years ago. He said that it was much more difficult than any other race he has run in. John does not exaggerate. The North African desert temperatures, combined with the difficulties of the terrain, carrying your own survival gear and the potential for danger make this daunting event unique.

THE WASHINGTON STATE CENTENNIAL SUPERMARATHON

A Tale of Two Cities opens with this line, "It was the best of times. It was the worst of times." That phrase would be quite appropriate for the Lewis and Clark Trail Run, aka the Washington State Centennial Run that went from Clarkston, WA, on the Idaho border, clear across the state of Washington to Cape Disappointment on the Pacific. Maybe I should have seen it as an omen that the orientation was held on April Fool's Day, 1989 and that the finish of the race was at Cape Disappointment. Even so, I doubt that I would have been smart enough to understand the signs of impending doom. Maybe, too, I should have been wary when race management decided after the start that there would be two different sets of super-marathon rules, the 'original' rules that required running the full 100 km per day within the previously set time limits, and the 'new' rules that said you could run as many miles as you wanted, any hours that you wanted to run: Take your pick and somehow get there. Hmmm.

While not a true super-marathon, the Washington State Centennial went in daily stages from the Washington-Idaho border to the Pacific Ocean. Almost all of the runners were in relay teams consisting of ten runners, each team member running 10 km daily, for a team total of 100 km per team per day. It took ten relay runners to do the daily 100 kilometers, but we were going to do it solo. A dozen of us decided, "*We are so damned tough that we don't need no stinkin' relay team; We can do all of it alone.*" We were determined that we could run each day's 100 kilometers, about 62 miles, as individual solo runners: *100 kilometers per day every day! What whack-jobs we were!* Most of us opted for the 'original' rules. We were all overambitious in our self assessments. The term *chutzpah* doesn't even come close. So if the race was actually *more than* a marathon each day, I guess that this event should be called a super-ultra-marathon for lack of a better term.

At the end of the first day, running west against a strong, humbling, steady headwind blasting up the Columbia Gorge (the ever present wind makes the Columbia Gorge one of the best wind-surfing places in the world), half of us super-heroes dropped out. At the end of the second 100 kilometer day there were only four of us left. Gary Wright and I dropped out after day three. (In the Hash House Harriers Gary is known as F'n-Crazy and I am F'n-Nuts. You'd have to be a Hasher to understand.) That left Jesse Dale Riley and Adrian Crane as the only two who would go on to finish the whole race, each finishing in first place due to two different sets of rules. Because I lasted three days, the race officials told me that I was in third place. I got a big wooden plaque shaped like the State of Washington. *Whoopee!* Being a drop-out isn't always so bad.

(I think that it was on day two that one of the runners wandered off course, got lost and roamed around aimlessly late at night. He was hungry, thirsty, incoherent and, according to Washington State Police, delusional. Not knowing who they had or what he was doing 'running around in his drawers at night' they put him in a mental facility until race officials found out where he was and arranged for his release.)

TOUR OF THE GOLDEN WEST: PRODUCING YOUR OWN SUPERMARATHON

There had never been a true super-marathon in North America. My experiences in Russia and France made me, as an American, a little envious: If people in those countries can put on their super-marathons, maybe we Americans can do it at home, maybe even better, and I plunged recklessly ahead with the project. I had no idea how difficult it would be.

A group of ultra-marathoner friends and I sat down for a brainstorming session. We wanted to put on an event that would showcase the best of our part of the country, the American West. We would take visiting runners to places that they would otherwise never get to see and would certainly never forget. Several members of our planning group were veterans of the Western States 100 Mile Run, a footrace that crosses the Sierra Nevada Mountains in dense, rugged forest. We love that race and its spectacular mountain setting. We agreed that our *Tour of the Golden West Super-Marathon* would have to take place in the Sierra Nevada.

It was our goal to put together a series of scenic marathon-distance runs in such a way that where one day's run finished, the next one would start. Most of the stages had to be on backwoods trails, starting at a roadside trailhead, and finishing where the trail terminated at another road, with at least one intermediate point for access to aid stations and for emergencies on the trail. For several months we travelled from our homes to the mountains, about four hours drive each way. We ran hundreds of miles of trails to scout out routes, discarding most for various reasons. The course that we eventually put together was brilliant. The first day would start on the Nevada side of the Sierras, south of Reno, and continue south through wild horse country and the Comstock Mother Lode silver mines, finishing at the little hamlet of Mound House (which consisted of three brothels), a few miles east of Carson City. The second day we planned to run from Mound House through Carson City, up and over the trails of the Carson Range, past Spooner Summit, onto the Tahoe Rim Trail, ending up at television's Ponderosa Ranch near the town of Incline Village. The third leg skirted the north end of Lake Tahoe on a bike path, then north along the Truckee River, ending at the old Squaw Valley Olympic ski resort. From Squaw Valley we would climb up to the Pacific Crest Trail and run north at an average elevation of 8,000 feet then descend to the spot east of Donner Lake where the Donner Party made carnivorous history in the 1800s. We scheduled to run a portion of the Western States Trail not far from its terminus in Auburn. All of the first stages were at altitudes of between 5,000 and 10,000 feet. Then we would leave the Sierras for the coastal range, run across the Dumbarton Bridge, the Stanford campus, the rugged, historic Dipsea Trail, run through Mill Valley, Sausalito and across the Golden Gate Bridge to a grand finale on the Marina Green in view of Alcatraz on the San Francisco waterfront.

If you have ever put on a running event anywhere you know that you have to obtain the permission of all of the federal, state and local governmental jurisdictions along your route, in addition to the owners of any private land you may cross. Every one of those agencies has its own requirements, and there is always paperwork to fill out. We had to deal with bureaucrats from many agencies along the way, cities (Auburn, San Francisco, Sausalito, Truckee, Carson City and Reno), the Bureau of Land Management, the Forest Service (four different offices), the Golden Gate Bridge Authority, state parks in Nevada and California, and private land owners. A few helpful officials winked and told us that we should just go ahead with our run, since our numbers would be small and would have no environmental impact. Other self-important, anal bureaucrats maintained a negative attitude, making it difficult to get the right forms or any information whatsoever. Finally, though, all of the necessary permits were in place. To give ourselves legal status we formed a club under the auspices of the Road Runners Clubs of America. We called ourselves *les Marathoniens de l'Aventure de Amerique*, to honor the French club that had hosted us in the Brittany super-marathon.

With the complexity of the event we knew that we would have to limit the number of runners. Word about our planned race got out through the wonderful and mysterious pipeline that connects like-minded people. Applications from prospective runners started arriving in May for the October 1992 race. They came from 19 countries and most were accompanied by a *curriculum vitae* describing the applicant's running accomplishments and telling us why we should allow them to enter. When we finished our selection process we had included eight Americans; one Canadian; one Iranian; One Brit; one Greek; two Poles; one Czech; two Hungarians; three Russians (one of them from Chechnya); one Kazakh; and one competitor from the Netherlands. Russian Vitali Koval had set the world record for 100 km. Iranian James Zarei had just won a 400 km race from Nagasaki to Hiroshima. With a Tower of Babel like that, one would expect major language problems, but most spoke some English, and I could communicate in basic Russian with the rest.

With all the twists and turns along so many miles of backwoods running trails we would need a lot of manpower to help along the way. As we had hoped, the running community came through, with volunteers from the San Francisco Hash House Harriers; Reno's Silver State Striders; the Palo Alto Running Club; DSE Runners; Tamalpa; the Sierra Express Running Club and The Orinda Road Runners. They would serve as trail markers, guides, pacers, man water stations, timers, logistics (food and housing) and, if runners got lost in the forest, organize search parties.

The runners flew into San Francisco. After we picked up the first group at SFO we took them on a mini tour of San Francisco while we waited for the rest to arrive. They oohed and aahed at "Everybody's Favorite City's" tourist attractions: the Golden Gate Bridge, Alcatraz and Fisherman's Wharf. Someone asked if we could drive through the Castro, San Francisco's gay heartland. One of the Russians marveled at the many beautiful women on the street. "I am falling in love every minute, so many magnificent women." To his embarrassment one of his countrymen straightened him out, "My friend, those girls that are so attractive to you, they are not girls. They are beautiful boys. I worry about you."

That first night 20 of them slept wherever they could find space on the floor of my home. We drove in a caravan of cars across the Sierra Nevada to Reno the next morning. In Reno we took a day to let the runners shake off their jet lag and acclimate to the 5,000 foot altitude. Reno's Silver State Striders graciously hosted us to both a 10 km prologue run and a tasty 'typical American' barbecue.

On the first official race day a few runners got slightly off trail in the high desert as we passed the abandoned Comstock Lode silver mines. Runners from the Silver State Striders got them back where they belonged quickly. The explanation was that ghosts from the Comstock days had moved the trail markers to protect their hidden stash of silver. Otherwise, miraculously, no one got lost. That day we ended our run in front of the Kit Kat Klub. We turned down the madam's invitation to come in and frolic with the professional ladies. A couple of the visiting runners were disappointed that I had not arranged for that kind of diversion.

With a moving group of hungry runners we had to find hearty and inexpensive food for them and for our sizeable support crew. You can't just barge into a restaurant with 50 very hungry people and expect instant seating and good service. All-you-can-eat buffets worked best, and by dealing with restaurant managers in the weeks ahead we were able to get favorable pricing and guaranteed seating. The first evening we were the guests of a casino buffet in Reno. When the Russians saw the large variety and high quality of the food they were stunned.

FLASHBACK. We are in a casino buffet for dinner. Marat Zhilanbaev, the Kazakh, looks at me and asks in Russian, "What are we allowed eat?" I tell him to take whatever he wants from the buffet tables.

He asks me about the quantity he can take, and I tell him that there is no limit. Eat whatever you want, as much as you want. His face reddens and his eyes become as big as saucers. He is angry. "This is what @#$%& Lenin promised to us Soviet citizens. We are still waiting for it after 70 years and you have had it all along." He takes his Communist Party internal passport from his pocket and slams it to the floor, stamping on it. Then he digs into the buffet with gusto. I kept his discarded Party card as a souvenir.

Night after night our famished marathon runners wreaked havoc on the profitability of Sizzler's, Denny's and whatever purveyor of food was unfortunate enough to get in our ravenous way. In Truckee we may have sent the local Sizzler's into bankruptcy. The sign said, "All you can eat," but they had not met our gang of hungry supermarathoners.

Finding one-night-stand housing for an itinerant gang of smelly runners was another big logistical problem. The first night all of them stayed in my home in Silicon Valley, sleeping on the floors, sofas, anywhere we could stack bodies before we drove up to the Sierras. On a few nights we were lucky enough to take over youth hostels. On a couple of occasions we stayed in hotels, special rates negotiated long ahead of time. The day we finished at the Ponderosa Ranch, the generous people of the community of Incline Village invited us to stay in their homes. It was a fine opportunity for the foreign runners to get to know American families.

The terrain was difficult, almost all of it on narrow trails, none of it flat, much of it at high altitude. A twisted ankle ten miles from nowhere was not a desired outcome, so we urged the runners to be very cautious. As a result, the marathon times were conservative. Most of the runners finished every stage, a few dropping out because of fatigue or minor injuries. Under such stressful conditions it always amazes me that the athletes remained calm and easy going.

There were incidents that brought a bit of levity to the group. After running on the Pacific Crest Trail, Marat, the runner from Kazakhstan reported that he had come across a black bear on the trail. They are quite common in the Sierra Nevada Mountains. When he was asked what he did about the bear, he replied, "Kazaks never afraid of bears. I kick him in *zhopa* and send him running. American bears not so tough like fierce Russian bears." One time a campus police officer caught Andres, a Hungarian runner, relieving himself in the trees as we crossed the Stanford campus. I happened to be there at the time. The officer was apoplectic and about to give the Hungarian a citation, so I intervened. "Officer, please let me handle this: he does not speak English." Then I turned to young Andres, who was actually fluent in English, waved a finger at him like a chastening mother, and warned sternly, "*No makee kaka!*" The cop almost choked on his laugh and Andres continued his run with no citation.

Our last day of running took us across the historic Dipsea Trail, site of the second oldest distance running race in America (behind the Boston Marathon.) It is a killer of a trail, seven miles of narrow, all up and down single track, with much treacherous footing along the way. Then we ran along bike paths through Mill Valley and Sausalito and over the Golden Gate Bridge to finish at San Francisco's Marina Green. The venerable Walter Stack was on hand to present awards. Andres Low ran so well day after day that he won the race overall with the best cumulative time. He averaged 3:02:43 for each mountain marathon, a remarkable pace considering the altitude, the difficult terrain, unfamiliarity with the trails and the fact that the runners got not a single rest day. The Kazakh, Marat Zhilanbaev, was second, Miklos Nemes, the other Hungarian was third and Ger Wijenberg from the Netherlands was fourth. The top American (8th place) was Stan Hardesty, a GI stationed in Germany.

Despite the difficulties of staging the event, I was sorry to see it end, and even sorrier to see the wonderful runners leave us to return home. One of the Russians confided that his wish was that there would be enough coal to keep his family warm for the oncoming harsh winter. In a few days of shared deep personal effort we had become a cohesive band, a tribe. We will never meet again, but neither will we forget our Golden West experience.

Our organizing group had reason to be very proud of the result of their effort. We had produced the first (and only, so far) true super-marathon in America, and we had done it with quite well. Runners went back home to their home countries to tell the tale. Some sent us copies of newspaper and magazine articles in Russian, Polish and Hungarian about our race. They would excite and stimulate other runners back home to want to come to America and run the superb *Tour of the Golden West*. But, you know what? *They can't*, because I am never going to go through all of that again. Nor, to this date, has anyone else.

Trans-Siberia: A wooden Catholic church built by Polish slave labor in Irkutsk.

In Siberia we often stayed at the Russian version of Boy Scout ("Pioneer") camps.

Crossing Siberia we passed several gulags.

A Canadian runner and a Russian runner along the BAM route in Siberia. The support bus is following in the distance.

In Siberian villages local people would sometimes join our run. Note the shabby Stalinist construction. We were the first foreigners that most of these people had ever seen.

Golden Circle: Running with a Russian military officer.

Golden Circle: Russian children helping Dutchman Ger Wijenberg draw water from a well.

Golden Circle: A single duck was shared by 20 of us. Fortunately I had a large jar of peanut butter to go with the good Russian black bread, downed with copious vodka.

Golden Circle: Along our route we passed one spectacular, historic church after another.

Golden Circle: After each day's marathon the teams got together to eat and chat. Here I am leading the group in a three-language version of Frere Jacques, English, French and Russian. I had to translate it into Russian.

Grand Course de Bretagne: I am ready for the start at Mont St. Michel, France.

Bretagne: Mont St Michel: "Runners to your marks, get set, ..."

Bretagne: About one fifth of the distance was along canals built by Napoleon.

The Bretons are a Celtic people. They play bagpipes and wear kilts. The language is closer to Welsh than French.

Bretagne: We were greeted royally in every village.

Bretagne: A village mayor welcoming us and giving us our awards.
Runners are Tom Possert, Joe Oakes, Stan Hardesty, Jo Wells and
Esmond Mah

Bretagne: Polish runners enjoying local French wine.

Bretagne: The Russian team did very well, were always ready for more punishing miles. Gennady Schvets is in the middle.

Bretagne: The locals were rather laid back.

Bretagne: Here I am joined by Jo Welles running into the next town.

Bretagne: Every morning the groaning board was set with a 'petit dejeuner' breakfast.

Bretagne: I am enjoying a big bowl of coffee as a guest in a French home.

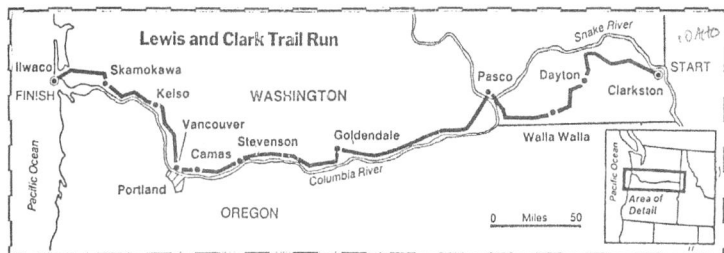

Washington Centennial Run: A map of the course from Idaho to the Pacific Ocean.

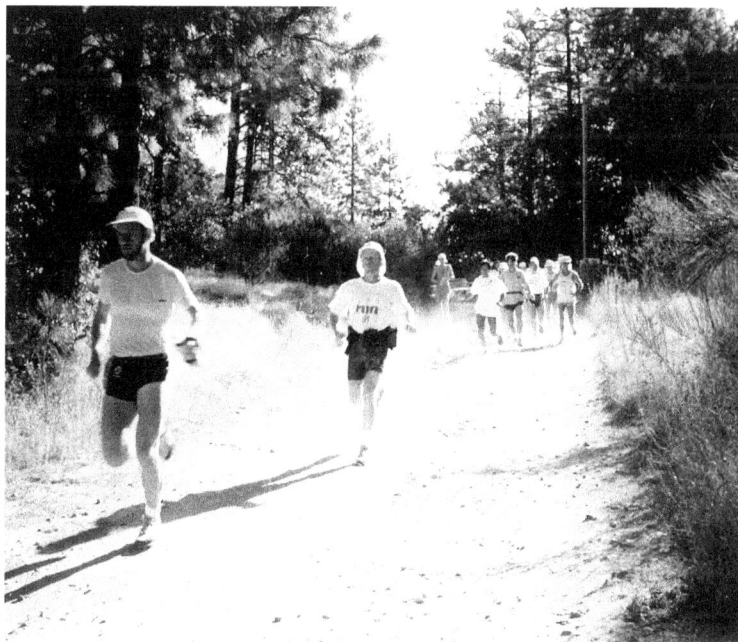

Tour of the Golden West Supermarathon: Ger Wijenberg (Holland) leads the pack in the first stage going south from Reno, Nevada.

TGW: Mike Tselentsis overtaking Jo Welles near an abandoned silver mine in the desert.

TGW: The immensity of the mountains becomes clear with a runner almost infinitesimally tiny on the high altitude Pacific Crest Trail.

TGW: We encountered deer and bears along our route.

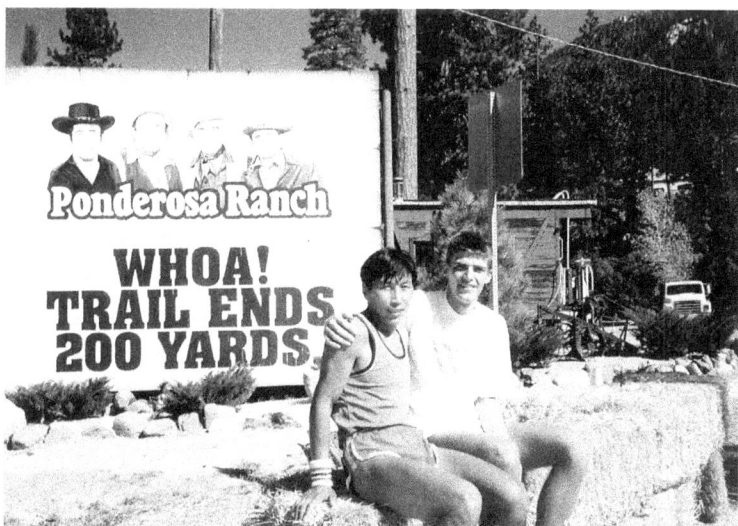

TGW: Marat Zhilanbaev (Kazakstan) and Andres Low (Hungary) at the end of the second marathon stage,

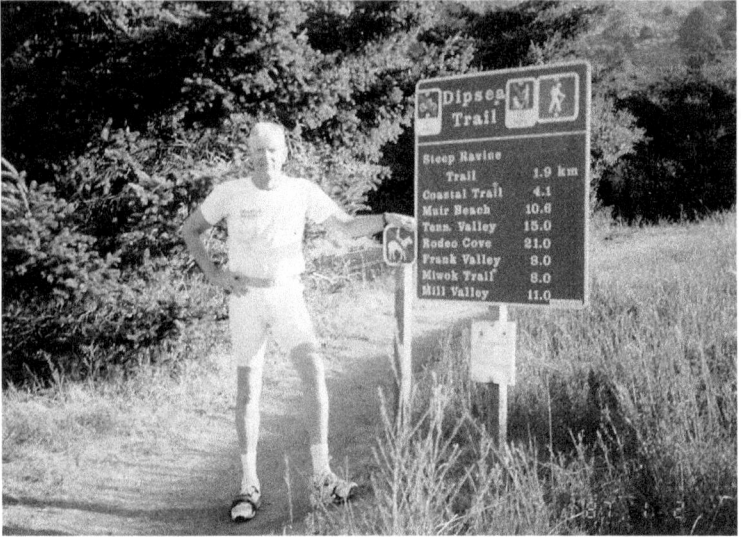

TGW: Ben Jones at the start of the final stage. That day the trail started by traversing the 11 km Dipsea Trail, then south into San Francisco via the Golden Gate Bridge.

TGW: Andres Low looks strong finishing in first place, even after all those marathons.

TGW: Marat "The Camel" Zhilanbaev was not far behind Andres Low.

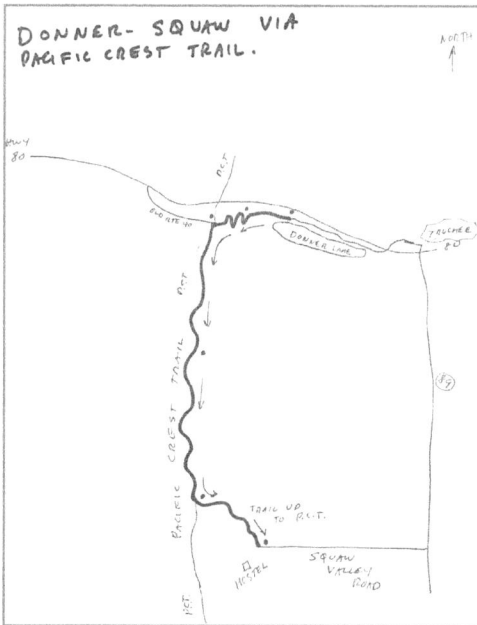

TGW: This is typical of the 'high-tech' course maps I made for the runners. On this one I accidentally had the arrows going backwards and had to explain the problem to the runners at the start.

167

More Running: There is Always More Running

"By trying hard we can easily learn to endure adversity. Another man's I mean."

– Mark Twain.

"A slow sort of country!" said the Queen. "Now, here, you see, it takes all the running you can do, to keep in the same place. If you want to get somewhere else, you must run at least twice as fast as that."

– Lewis Carroll, Alice's Adventures in Wonderland

"No road is too long for advances deliberately and without undue haste; and no honors are too distant for the man who prepares himself for them with patience."

– Bruyere

I have a tattoo on my right forearm. It reads *potikhonko*, a Russian word meaning "Take it easy." It is a reminder that if I push too hard I am going to come to a bad end quickly. The Italians have a way of saying the same thing: *Chi va piano, va lontano e sano. Chi va forte, va alla morte.* Go peacefully and you will go long and in good health; push yourself and you will die. That is the crux of my training philosophy: I want to be able to continue to train without injuring myself, tomorrow, next month and for the rest of my life.

CHAPTER EIGHT:
MORE RUNNING: THERE"S ALWAYS MORE RUNNING

JOURNEY RUNS

A journey run is much like a super-marathon in that you run very far every day, but your objective is to get from A to B, someplace much further away than 26 miles. The difference is that the daily distance of a journey run is whatever the organizer (who might be yourself) decides, and any day's run might be longer or shorter than a marathon. It can be a solo undertaking or an organized event. Journey runs were fairly common over a century ago in both the USA and Britain. They were called 'pedestrian' or go-as-you-please races, and big money was often involved. The most famous of them went from New York to Los Angeles, and a man named Weston won several large purses for his efforts. And then there was Forrest Gump.

More recently Alan Firth, an Englishman living in North Carolina, directed a race that went in the opposite direction, The Run Across America, from Los Angeles to New York. I was at the start in LA a few years back, marveling at the level of fitness and the depth of dedication that it would take these rugged runners to average over 40 miles a day, week after week for about two months. Firth's runners came from several countries. Each day he prepared a route map for them with detailed instructions for the day's journey. Think about the amount of preparation that goes into planning and scouting a new route every day for months, including finding places for the athletes to sleep and eat. Consider what it might be like to worry about the location and health of a spread-out group of runners, some of whom speak limited English. It is like moving an army. Alan and Mary Firth put on that run for several years for financial no return, dedicating months of their lives to the effort. They are among the unsung saints of the running world. While we are talking about Alan and Mary Firth, they both did an exceptional journey run in Britain. It started at John O'Groats on the northern tip of Scotland and went all the way to the southeastern extremity of England, a place called Land's End.

Some runners do journey runs on their own, often for a cause. A young cancer patient named Terry Fox started running from his home in western Canada, intending to run all the way across Canada to Nova Scotia. His daily progress made the evening news all over Canada. Terry's cancer defeated him before his goal. He died en route, but his great effort captivated his countrymen. The net result was an increase in awareness of cancer and large donations toward cancer research, given in his name. There is a cairn and a plaque dedicated to Terry Fox on a pleasant rise above Nanisivik on Baffin Island. A few years after Terry Fox's effort, Canadian Jo Welles ran his route in reverse, going east to west. She made it all the way to her goal in British Columbia.

I knew ultra-runner Brian Robinson when he was a teenage Boy Scout growing up in Northern California. After several years working as an engineer in Silicon Valley he found himself with sufficient leisure time and the means to pursue a very special goal. Brian completed the entire lengths of the Appalachian Trail, the Continental Divide Trail and the Pacific Crest Trails, amazingly, all three in one calendar year. Most experienced backpackers are happy to hike ten miles a day. Brian averaged 29 miles a day for almost a year, carrying everything he needed to live and keep moving in the mountains. His journey took him across torrid areas of Southern California and snow-covered mountain ranges in the Sierra Nevada, the Rockies and the Appalachians. What he accomplished was like going from Mexico to Canada, back to Mexico and back to Canada again on foot. No one else has ever managed to do that in one calendar year.

One of the most interesting journey runs goes from Melbourne to Sydney in Australia, a distance of about 1,000 kilometers. When

Cliff Young won it several years ago he became a national hero. Everyone knew his name. "He's that farmer who trains in his gum boots." A multiple winner of that event was unbelievably talented a Greek emigree to Australia. Many believe that Yannis Kouris is the best ultramarathon runner ever to live. They might be right.

Being talented and winning long races does not guarantee fame. It helps if you are good at getting press coverage. Another talented ultrarunner and journey runner is Dean Karnazes, a San Franciscan who is excellent at working with the media. Besides being a good runner, he is good at writing about it. His book, *Ultraman*, is worth perusing.

12, 24 AND 48 HOUR RUNS

These are just what they sound like: the clock determines when the race ends, not a specific distance. These events are usually contested on a track, where runners get in as many laps as possible during the duration of the run. The fact that they are held in a confined space makes it easy to control. Food, drinks, toilet facilities, medics, etc. are never far from the runners, and there is no need to worry about runners interfacing with motor vehicles. The downside is that it is like swimming laps in a pool: without a change of scenery it can get quite boring. I have participated in a few of these runs, using them for long distance training for ultramarathons. My goals were modest. In a 12 hour run 100 km would be a very good goal for me, but anything over 50 miles was acceptable. My favorite 12 hour run was put on by the San Francisco DSE Runners on a half mile dirt track in Golden Gate Park. When the 12 hour finish horn goes off, runners stop in place so their final partial lap can be measured. Less common are 24 hour runs, and even less so are 48 hour runs. Don Choi, a mail deliverer, set a US record for 48 hours on a track in Burlingame, CA. The amazing Don did much of his training by running his mail route carrying his sack of letters. I was told that his union shop steward was a bit put out that he did his route in half the allotted time. (There is the bad joke about the runner who tried to set a personal best for the 24 hour run by finishing in 23 hours.)

THE MILLENNIUM RUN THAT NEVER HAPPENED

In 1998 Arctic Joe Womersley and I had the bright idea to put on an extremely long relay run that would go all the way from the far north of Canada south to the bottom of Chile. Hundreds of local runners would be involved in their home area all along the route. Some of them might want to be involved for the entire journey. It was to supposed take place in the months leading up to New Years Day of the Millennium Year, 2,000. The run would start during the Canadian summer and finish in the Chilean summer five months later. We calculated the road distances and days of running for each leg of the journey, and it worked out as follows:

COUNTRY	KILOMETERS	DAYS OF RUNNING
Canada	3,800	24
USA (WA, OR, CA)	3048	22
Mexico	3827	24
Central America	2367	16 (Guat., el Salv., Hond., Nica, C' Rica and Pan.)

(We allowed three off days to get around the impassable Darien Gap between Panama and Columbia.)

Columbia	1142	7
Ecuador	859	6
Peru	2602	17
Chile	5295	32 (Includes some of Argentina plus two ferry days.)

It was scheduled to start August 1 in Inuvik, the northernmost town reachable by road in Canada, and finish in Puntarenas, Chile on December 31 in time for the big hoopla of the Millennium on January 1, 2000, when all computers were supposed to crash and the electronic-dependent world was supposed to grind to a halt.

We made contact with running clubs and local authorities all along the route. Almost everyone was anxious to help us and wanted to be part of it. We had runners clambering to be members of the relay team. Arctic Joe and I spent months getting ready for it.

It was a great idea, but it never came off. *Why didn't it happen?* Kidnapping had become a cottage industry in Columbia and in parts of Peru. No insurance company would consider covering us, and Arctic Joe and I could not personally cover the risk. End of project.

Things have gotten worse since then, especially in Mexico. I don't think that anyone will ever be able to pull it off. But, hey, *why the heck not?*

Not all ideas end with a successful conclusion. But if you do not at least dream, your sofa cushions will start to feel more and more like a part of you.

RUNNING ONE MILE PER HOUR

This story is based on an article I researched for ULTRARUN-NING MAGAZINE. Several years ago I read about a most unusual event that was held in Los Angeles in the year 1910. It involved a race in which a runner was required to run only one mile per hour, but had to run his one mile in each of many, many consecutive hours, skipping not a single hour. That meant running 24 miles per day, with one mile in every single one of the 24 hours. Why would anyone do that? The winner was promised a purse of $1,000, an enormous sum in 1910.

Participants were allowed to sleep, eat or leave the building, as long as they logged their mile on the track during each and every hour on the clock. If they missed completing a full mile during any hour they were out of the race, finished. Hundreds showed up at the start. There were many who made it through the first 24 hours, and a lesser number after 48 hours. Not many made it beyond three days.

The biggest problem was sleep deprivation. The best strategy was to run and finish a mile just before the end of an hour, then immediately run another mile a few minutes later after the beginning of the next hour. That gave the runner about 100 minutes in between, to grab a nap and eat before having to run again. They kept it up until they could run no more hourly miles. In 1910 the recognized world record for the event was 614 miles, in other words 614 hours. A man named Eugene Estoppy, a Swiss-American living in Venice, California, told the world that he could top the record. He boasted that he would, in fact, run 1,000 hourly miles in 1,000 consecutive hours. To show that he meant it, he went to the bookmakers and placed a $1,000 bet on himself.

On November 20, 1910 Eugene Estoppy ran his first mile on a board track in a dance hall, 12 laps to the mile. His goal was to continue running a mile every hour until the stroke of midnight, New Year's Eve, 1911. Not only did he succeed, but it is recorded that he ran many of his miles quite fast, including one at 4:20, which was a West Coast record for the mile at that time. He broke the existing world record by more than 50%, running his miles every hour for more than 40 days. Eugene Estoppy had earned his $1,000 the hard way. The newspapers also record that he was paid an additional $200 to run one more mile on New Year's Day at the Pasadena Tournament of Roses.

That kind of race has not been contested in about a century. Someone should organize a one-mile-per-hour race. I am wondering if, perhaps I might ……. Never mind, it sounds like a whole lot of work.

THE WILDWOOD TRAIL

My favorite running haven is Portland, Oregon's 5,000 acre Forest Park, the largest urban park in the USA. Thank God that there is never enough money for the city to 'develop' the park.

Forest Park is on the northeastern slope of a long ridge of land that hovers above Portland and her western suburbs. Because of the canopy of tall trees, running is always cool in Forest Park. On the wider trails, like Ericson and Saltzman, being in the shelter of the forest is like passing through a long and welcoming cathedral. Occasional patches of brilliant sunlight find openings through the trees and I become temporarily dazzled by the light.

There are 20 steep, narrow side trails, many of them connecting the upper part of the ridge with the lower elevations, some linking the higher Wildwood Trail with the Ericson below. These vertical side trails are very rough, with roots and rocks every step. Care must be taken to keep one's speed in check when running downhill. So I slow down.

The main north-south trail is the Wildwood Trail, which extends a full 50 kilometers from the Oregon Zoo on the south to Newberry Road on the north extremity of the park. En route there are only three roads to cross, Burnside Road, Cornell Road and Germantown Road. For much of its length the Wildwood Trail is about a foot wide, with heavy vegetation on both sides. At the bases of the old trees, ferns spring up everywhere and moss covers the disintegrating remnants of fallen giants. There are no long flat stretches. The Wildwood Trail winds in and out of a hundred gullies, many of them crossed by narrow wooden bridges. The tall trees keep the sun at bay and traffic is light. I normally encounter very few runners or hikers. In rainy weather parts of the trail can be slick.

As I run north along the wider Ericson Trail, there is a profusion of enormous ferns growing out of the steep wall to my left, thousands of them, living among the moss-covered tree trunks: they seem to be watching me, silent, as I pass by. When a breeze penetrates the forest, the ferns do a football stadium 'wave' and I want to think that they are cheering me on. The Ericson Trail was created many years ago to provide access to an ill-advised housing development in the park. It proved to be impossible because of the steep, rugged terrain. But the cut that they made through the forest affords peaceful access, with only an occasional mountain biker feeling his oats as he careers though this wild domain. There is no motor traffic on the Ericson Trail, the Saltzman Road Trail or any trail in Forest Park.

FLASHBACK. I am running downhill on the Saltzman Road Trail. To my left the land falls off sharply. To my right is a carved wall that was created when this dirt road was bulldozed many years ago. On the uphill side the trees, high above me, have pushed their ghostly roots down through the cut away soil and out into the open air, forming a lattice-work fence of exposed roots, blindly and hungrily trying to find their way back into the soil. On my left side the nearby trees fly by me quickly, as if I am watching them from a car window. In the background the distant trunks sullenly stand their ground, quietly spying from their cover.

It is winter, the rainy season in the Pacific Northwest. That means that the side trails are going to be muddy, slippery, so caution is called for. There are places on those trails where storm-downed trees have to be hurdled, and some stretches have been washed out, dragging tons of earth down the mountain towards the Columbia River. But the weather has little effect on the Saltzman Trail.

After two miles I reverse my direction, now running back uphill on Saltzman. Today I will conclude my workout with uphill intervals. I run fast for 40 breaths, 160 steps, and slow down for ten breaths. The first set is hard and I am sucking wind. The next set is even harder. A mile and a half of intervals is plenty. After six sets I walk the rest of the way uphill to my car. I feel as though I have done something good for myself.

The mascot of the University of California at Santa Cruz is the banana slug. Santa Cruz is on the rainy side of California's Coastal Range, but it has nothing on Portland when it comes to 'liquid sunshine'. During the wet season, roughly five months of the year, I will wager that the banana slugs along our trails are more prolific, bigger and slimier than Santa Cruz's iconic banana slugs. Maybe we should challenge Santa Cruz to a slug competition.

THE NIKE LOOP

My second favorite place to run locally is the Nike Loop. Nike Corporation, headquartered in Beaverton, Oregon, had the foresight to build a landscaped running trail encircling their beautiful campus, almost two miles long. It is a pleasant place to run, open to the public, with convenient access and good street parking. What I like most about it is that the wood-chip surface makes for comfortable running for these creaky old bones. The four short hills are gentle and there are overpasses to cross access roads. Part of the trail is under well groomed trees. There is variety of lush landscaping, including rose gardens. I often slow down at the three ponds along the trail, where tired migratory waterfowl linger for a while in the spring and fall.

Nike generously supports local runners in addition to the stable of top-flight distance runners that make up what is called The Oregon Project. Once in a while one of those gazelles flies past me like a bullet. At their level, training is a full time job. I sincerely hope that these young runners will learn to love their sport as I have, and keep at it for many years to come.

As I run around the Loop I try to hold in my mind what it was like to run fast and free like these young lions, to feel the wind in my face as I move like a deer. I do remember what it was like, and I really can relive the sensations. My precious memories!

FLASHBACK: It seems like only yesterday, because it was only yes-

terday. Early November is probably the best time of the year for runners in Oregon. The heavy winter rains have not yet arrived, the cool air makes it perfect for running, and when the sun is shining the days are glorious.

Yesterday as I ran the Nike Loop I was reminded again about what I love about my sport. I was feeling a little guilty about running when there were things that needed to be done at home. About 100 yards into the run, on the west side of the loop, a fat beaver-like nutria was mowing the grass beside the trail, busily stuffing his face. He couldn't care less about me gawking at him. A few hundred yards further on there was another nutria, this one a mother with three little ones, all of them busily mowing Nike's grass. Little nutrias look like fat bunnies. I left them to their mowing. On the north side of the loop there is a bridge that crosses a long, man-made waterfall, flanked on both sides by trees in full, brilliant autumn colors. I stopped long enough to record a mental image and moved on. When I made the turn onto the east side of the loop a flock of geese swooped over my head and landed on the grassy slope in front of me, where they, too, did their part in mowing Nike's lawns.

If I had stayed home to do my chores, I would have missed all of that. The work can wait. Many years ago a pair of Russian writers, Ilff and Petrov, travelled across North America and wrote about their journey. One sentiment, roughly translated, stands out for me: "You can always find time for your work, but your chances to enjoy the smell of a field of clover are rare and must be grasped and appreciated instantly." I find my fields of clover in my running. There is always something new waiting for me just around the corner. How lucky can you get?

CROSSING THE
FINISH LINE

"And in the end it is not the years in your life that count. It is the life in your years." Abraham Lincoln

I no longer run marathons. Ultra-marathons and super-marathons are things of the past for me. After 130 marathons and 51 ultras, I am not sure that I would want to run another one even if it were still in my power. But, of course, it is not. Perhaps that sounds like sour grapes, but I think it is just contentment that comes from acceptance of reality. I did what I could while I could do it: there is no room for regret. I am satisfied. I still run a little, but just as important, I have so many fine memories that I can savor and share.

ONE SHINING, MEMORABLE KILOMETER

After more than six decades of running I am sometimes asked if there is one memory about my running that I cherish above all others. The answer is yes, and it happened in the spring of 1996. After the completion of my non-motorized circumnavigation of the earth (see below), I was selected by my community, the City of Mountain View, California, to carry the Olympic Torch in what was called the 'Community Heroes Program.'

I was in good company: Along with me, Olympians John Powell (discus and shot put) and Peggy Fleming (ice skating) also took their one kilometer turns carrying the torch that morning. It was on its way to the Olympic Games in Atlanta via a circuitous route that allowed hundreds of lucky Americans to experience the honor and thrill of carrying the Olympic flame for one kilometer near their homes.

Both sides of broad El Camino Real were lined crowded with

people who had come to see the Olympic Torch passing through our town. They were on rooftops, sitting on cars and trucks, several deep along the sidewalks, cameras in hand. Flags were waving and people were jumping and cheering. Fathers hoisted children onto their shoulders so they could see something that their little ones might remember all their lives: the Olympic Torch being carried through Mountain View, a once in a lifetime experience. Kids were climbing trees and street lamps. A few yards in front of me, straddling the center of the road, was a 14 vehicle police motorcycle escort. Ahead of us in the right lane were media vehicles, TV cameras whirring, newspaper photographers jockeying to get pictures. A young companion was assigned to run next to me to catch the torch in the event that I faltered, and there was an alternate torchbearer in a van behind us to take over if necessary. *It was imperative that the Olympic torch keep moving forward. For this one kilometer that responsibility was mine.*

I tried to keep all of that out of my mind. My assignment was clear: to proudly display the Olympic flame to the people in my town and to advance its progress a little further towards Atlanta. The torch felt as light as a feather and I held it high so those in the back could get a glimpse of the flickering red and yellow flame. I knew that I was carrying everybody's torch, not just for my Mountain View neighbors, and not just for Californians or Americans. The Olympic ideals bind us together with everyone in today's world and with generations past and future. People will always be inspired by the traditions and ideals of the Olympic Games. *Fortius, altius, certius: Stronger, higher, faster,* is the command given to athletes, asking them to offer their very best.

That is my most cherished memory of a long life of running, even though it lasted only a few minutes. I cannot think of any better way of saying 'Thank you' to the many people who helped and inspired me during more than six decades of running than to carry that torch in their names.

To a young runner I offer this: Enjoy putting your body through its paces: pay your dues. Push yourself, but make sure to keep your running joyful. Feel the cool wind in your face and grasp the solid earth with your feet as you race toward your finishing line. Pay attention to the magnificent vistas that you encounter along the way and be ready for whatever may be around the next bend: the autumn colors, the play of the light through the trees, maybe a deer or a snail on the trail. Cultivate the camaraderie of moving along the surface of the earth with friends. Appreciate the awesome knowledge that the earth is really yours to traverse as far as your legs and lungs will take you: Know that they can take you a lot further than you realize. This is how our ancestors moved from Africa to all parts of the world. Running is not always easy, but if you have a love affair with it, the rough parts will be much smoother.

WHERE ARE THEY NOW?

I celebrated my 78th birthday on September 7, 2012. One of the sad facts too well known to us older folks is that we find ourselves losing so many of our friends. The longer you live the more of them who will leave you. Allow me to take a minute to salute departed friends from my running life: Coach Borck, Walter Stack, Peter Butler, Arctic Joe Womersley, Ron Kovacs, Colonel Len Wallach, Jerry Meyer, Fred Lebow, USMC Col. Buck Swannock, and so many others with whom I shared a mile, a marathon and a beer or two. They are gone, but I can call them up from my heart just by going out on the quiet trails to run alone for a while. They are at my side. I hear Walt Stack telling an off-color story (bleep) on the Johnny Carson show; Coach Howie is shouting workouts across the field at Macomb's Dam Park; The sad Sunday morning running in San Francisco DSE race with Peter Butler while his entire neighborhood in the Oakland Hills was in flames; Peter lost everything that morning. Arctic Joe urging the ultra-marathoners to moon the busload of 'wimpy' marathoners as their bus passed us on Baffin Island; Ron Kovacs explaining about pushing first through physical exhaustion, then getting past mental exhaustion, finally digging even deeper into his spiritual reserves to set an age group record for 50 miles; Sarlik Abramovich, who was recently murdered in Moscow, a warm and reliable friend, cautioning me to take it easy; tough Len Wallach treating me with tenderness when I couldn't get beyond my limits at Badwater. As long as memories of friends live, those friends also live. If there is a trail in Heaven set aside for runners, that is where I hope to join them all again, providing that I am allowed to enter.

Others, givers like George Rehmet, Sue Free, Kevin Lee, Jane Colman (DSE) and Jeff Wehrman (ORRC) continue with their generous gifts of time and energy, making the world of running a fuller, better place for all of us. Many more old friends are still with us, and that is reason to be thankful. Last year I visited with Gennady Schvetz and Nail "The Hammer" Bairamgalin in Moscow, strong and healthy, but not getting on well in the chaotic Putin kleptocracy.

John Warren's beautiful daughters have made him eternal by giving him multiple grandchildren. If nature is kind, the children will inherit the intellect and gentleness of beloved Sasquatch, but not his feet. There are few kinder people than runner Sandra Puanini Burgess in Honolulu. Barry (Hillside Straggler) Bettman, Cissy (Mammaries) Chase, Derek (Derelict) Eliot, Plucky, Headset, Cummin' Mutha, and many of the SF Hash House Harriers are still making trouble as often as they can. I am pleased to remain in contact with my former partners, friends forever, Gary Emich and Sally Bailey. And here is something great: new friends keep popping up, like Peggy and Allan Hubacker in Honolulu.

In this physical world of running, there is the literary side to keep us informed and amused. Among the leaders among the scribes are Joe Henderson, Rich Benyo and John Medinger, all of them fine runners and all dedicated journalists. The mystical running guru, Dr. George Sheehan is no longer with us, but his inspirational words will live on for many years to come. Each of them has had a positive influence on me over the years.

Others have long ago disappeared from my view, and I would dearly like to know where they are and how they are faring. Danny Roselli was last seen in London a few years back. Irving Rattner, the indefatigable inspiration of our CCNY night school track team, has surely retired from the US Government by now. I bet that he is still running (or hobbling) someplace, maybe in Florida. Has anyone seen Irv?

So very many good friends, some scattered, others gone, a few still active, too many unknown. How very lucky I have been to have had the chance to brush up against all of them. A long life of running has brought me so much happiness in the company of good friends.

To my former running mates I offer this: Run on and cherish what you still can do. Relish the memories of what is behind us. Have no regrets. You were there and you were in the game.

May I offer a free floating *Thank You for all the good memories*, widely broadcast to old friends, wherever they may be, and whomever it might reach?

I think that I have hit the wall. So, in closing, let us consider the words of that great philosopher, Dr. Seuss:

Don't cry because it's over. Smile because it happened.

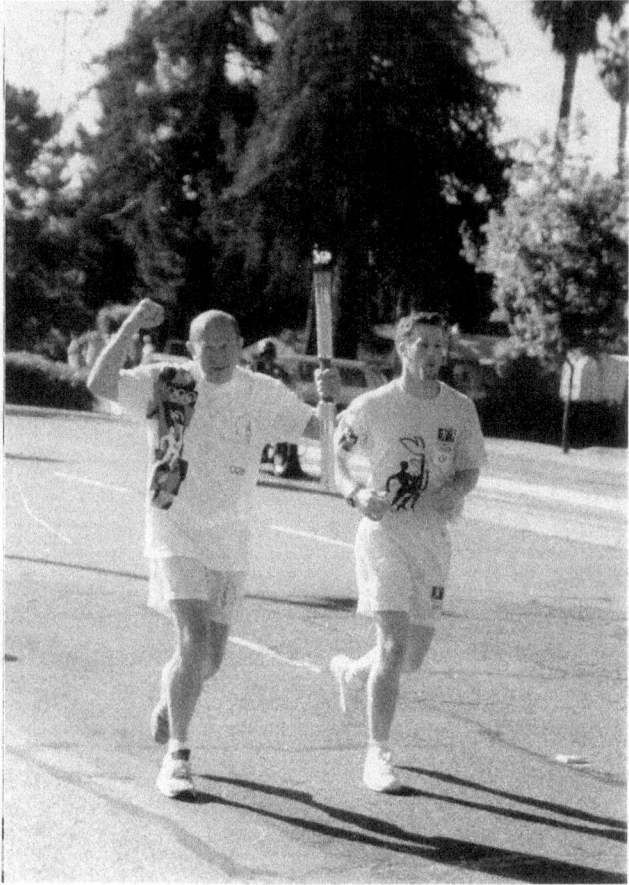

I was honored to carry the Olympic Torch for one kilometer as it passed through my town, Mountain View, CA.

Congress of the United States
House of Representatives
Washington, D. C. 20515

Anna G. Eshoo
Fourteenth District
California

April 30, 1996

Mr. Joseph Andrew Oakes
1359 Cuernavaca Circle
Mountain View, California 94035

Dear Mr. Oakes,

Congratulations on being chosen as a Community Hero Torchbearer for the 1996 Olympic Torch Relay. Your extraordinary generosity to the community qualifies you in a unique way for this honor and I salute you for it.

All my best,

Anna G. Eshoo
Member of Congress

AGE:ma

A congratulatory letter from my congressional representative, Anna G. Eshoo.

Confeteor

In the Catholic religion there is a prayer called The Confeteor, a prayer of confession. I have a confession to my readers: I am a bigamist. Throughout this book I have professed my great love for the sport of running, and it was all said in truth. The fact is, however, that I have another love.

Ever since I was a teenager I have been a swimmer, although competitive swimming never interested me. I have swum in places like the English Channel, the Strait of Gibraltar, the Bering Strait, and many times on what I consider my home court, Alcatraz.

So there you have it. I am enamored of both Mme Running and Mme Aqua. I have been unfaithful to my first and true love. But here is the best part: as I age, I take great comfort in the fact that Mme. Aqua does not do harm to my lower extremities: no pounding. Because I swim, I can keep myself fit with a combination of swimming and less running mileage. That's not so bad, is it?

Okay, the real truth is that I have had other flings, with bicycling, kayaking, dog mushing, you name it. Even jumping out of airplanes. But they have been just that … flings.

Finally, a goodby to running

On September 7, 2012, my 78th birthday, I entered Glendale Adventist Hospital for surgery on my knees, both of them. For too long, my beloved knees had been slowly degenerating, failing me, not allowing me the pleasure of running, leaving me in a great deal of pain, sometimes giving out on a downhill run. The good doctors told me that I would never be able to run again, with or without surgery. I got second and third opinions, confirming the diagnosis. They studied my x-rays and MRIs, and the graphic evidence was strong. *"Bone on bone. Those knees are shot. Replace them."* they said glumly and sternly, *"Do not even think of running."* Reluctantly, I came to agree with them.

There was nothing new about the medics telling me not to run. That was the advice given to me by an orthopedic surgeon at Stanford Sports Medicine Clinic, 32 years ago in 1980. He did arthroscopic surgery on first my right knee, then my left, because I had trashed the meniscus in both of them. About ten years ago another doctor told me the same thing: "Joe, you have to stop running!" Then he gave me a series of three injections with some glop that we hoped would relieve the pain and give me a bit more mobility. It worked for a few months, but not very well. I kept running.

Many runners hang up their sneakers after competing in school. Others stay with the sport (or later join it) and keep running until it finally loses its luster. Some eventually get tired of the pounding and stress-related injuries that are all too common among runners and throw in the towel. (Plantar fasciaitis; shin splints; stress fractures; muscle injuries; foot and most frequently, knee, ankle, back or hip problems, you name it.) I kept on running until I had squeezed the last drops from my sport. In retrospect, I have no doubt that I hung on too long. Then again, I have outlived some of the doctors who advised me not to run. I have had many years of pleasure and have enjoyed a level of good health that most non-runners dream of. I have no regrets; it was worth all the time, the effort, and yes, the pain.

My reasoning for opting for surgery was like this: I knew that I would never really be able to run well again, with or without surgery, so why put up with pain? Why should I live with decreased mobility? I could have chosen to take pain killers, but developing that kind of addiction has no appeal for me. My six decades of competitive running should be more than enough for anyone. It was finally the right time to hang up the running shoes and look at whatever the next phase of my life might offer; perhaps it will be very interesting. And that is where I am now, healing and exploring my options. After two months the healing is going well. I got rid of my walker after three weeks, and the cane went two weeks later. I am in love with the exercise bicycle that is helping me regain knee flexibility.

Alexander Graham Bell is quoted as saying, *"When one door closes another one opens; but we too often look so long and regretfully upon the closed door that we do not see the ones that open for us."* Like a kid before Christmas, I am anxious to take a peek through that next door.

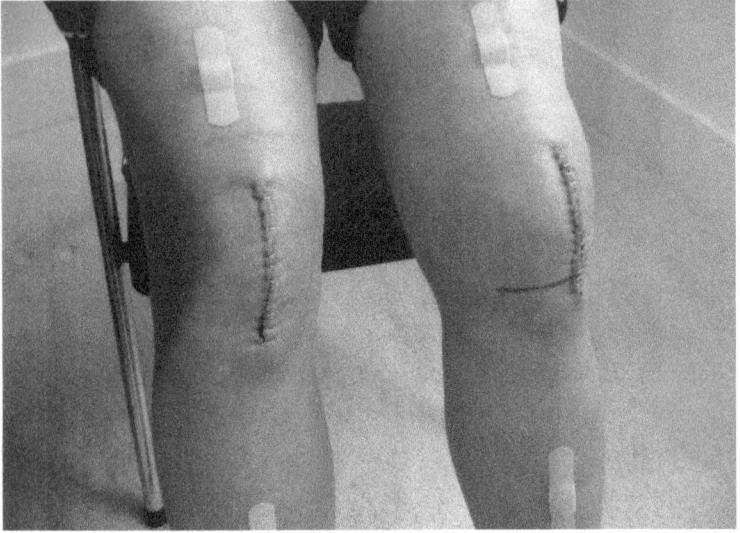

There are new knees under those 42 titanium staples. The staples were removed ten days after surgery.

Index

194